TRUTH MATTERS

A Dialogue on Fruitful Disagreement
in an Age of Division

T0321301

ROBERT P. GEORGE
& CORNEL WEST

Post Hill
PRESS

A POST HILL PRESS BOOK

ISBN: 979-8-88845-170-0
ISBN (eBook): 979-8-88845-171-7

Truth Matters:
A Dialogue on Fruitful Disagreement in an Age of Division
© 2025 by Robert P. George and Cornel West
All Rights Reserved

Cover design by Jim Villaflores

This is a work of nonfiction. All people, locations, events, and situations are portrayed to the best of the author's memory.

Post Hill Press
New York • Nashville
posthillpress.com

Published in the United States of America
1 2 3 4 5 6 7 8 9 10

To our teachers and students

These provocative, wide-ranging conversations were recorded in New York City in three sessions during the fall of 2023 and spring of 2024. In prompting and directing the discussion, emphasis was placed upon relating current issues to deeper questions of knowledge, faith, the search for truth and common ground, and the vocation of the teacher in the context of the modern university. The publisher wishes to thank Professors George and West for their generous participation in this project, as well as Nic Rowan, who assisted in the preparation of the manuscript.

Table of Contents

Chapter One

Seeking Truth Through Conversation

The two of you have been interviewed many times on the subject of your remarkable friendship and your long history of teaching together at Princeton. But for the benefit of those who don't know the story, why don't you tell us how you met.

Robert P. George: I felt a fellowship with Cornel even before we became friends because we were interested in the same questions. In Princeton faculty conversations, he was always insisting that the discussion—even if it would sometimes get a bit technical—come back to the important and deep questions, the questions of meaning and value. Once or twice we got together for lunch, but that was episodic and while we had nice conversations, we had not yet developed something we would count as a friendship, much less the deep relationship we later came to enjoy.

That friendship began in 2005 through a student of mine who was also a student of Cornel's. He showed up at my door during office hours to tell me about a project that he was involved with, creating a new campus magazine. He described it as our Princeton campus equivalent of *The New Yorker*. He and some of his fellow students had raised a large sum of money, I'm guessing from alumni, or in any event from friends, to launch it. He told me that in each issue, he wanted to have a feature where one Princeton professor would interview another. They had lined up Cornel West as interviewer in the inaugural issue and had asked him whom he would like to interview. Cornel had indicated he wanted to interview Robert George. "Who, me?" I asked.

I was flattered because, after all, Cornel could have chosen any faculty member; Princeton is filled with accomplished, celebrated scholars across a wide range of fields. Even then, I knew the breadth of Cornel's interests, from literature and art to philosophy. He could have interviewed anybody. Of course, I agreed to do it. When the appointed day came, we had the interview, if I can call it that. It was a rollicking, rambunctious conversation. It wasn't anything that I would recognize as an interview, but it was great. We talked about deep philosophical questions and contemporary political questions. It became very clear—even clearer than it previously had been—that we really were interested in the same sorts of issues.

I think it became clearer in that conversation that we were also interested in many of the same authors, the great philosophers of antiquity—Plato, Aristotle, Cicero—as well as medieval thinkers—Saint Augustine and Saint Thomas Aquinas—Reformation thinkers, Renaissance thinkers—Erasmus and Thomas More—Enlightenment thinkers, nineteenth-century figures such as John Henry Newman and John Stuart Mill, and twentieth-century thinkers, ranging from John Dewey to C.S. Lewis, and from Leo Strauss to Martin Luther King Jr. We read the same stuff, and the writers who shaped and influenced our thinking were in so many cases the same writers.

That conversation, which I think was supposed to be an hour or maybe two hours, ended up being more than four hours before I realized that I needed to get home for dinner. And even then, as we walked down to my car, we continued the conversation. I stood there for a half hour with my hand on the door latch because we couldn't stop chatting about these issues and thinkers we were both interested in. When we parted, we both said, "This has just been a wonderful conversation. We really do need to get to know each other better. Let's look for another opportunity to go to lunch or have dinner soon and continue the conversation."

But then, just a few days later, we both received a message from the dean of the college pleading for senior faculty to volunteer to teach freshman seminars. The freshman seminar program, she explained, was a very important part of our curriculum. We advertised it to prospective students, especially the fact that even freshmen at Princeton have opportunities to interact with senior faculty, even some of our most distinguished and celebrated faculty. But she needed more senior faculty to make that a reality. Well, the light bulb went off over my head: I recalled that conversation, which I'd had only a few days earlier with Cornel. I thought, "Wouldn't it be wonderful if Cornel and I could do a freshman seminar together focused on the great books that have shaped our own journeys, our intellectual and spiritual odysseys?"

I got in touch with Cornel, and he immediately said it was a great idea. So, we volunteered to teach our seminar. We called it "Adventures of Ideas," which is the title of one of the great Harvard philosopher Alfred North Whitehead's books. We began with Sophocles' *Antigone* and then read Plato's *Gorgias*, which had been a very important reading for my own development. We read Saint Augustine's *Confessions* and went all the way up to the twentieth century with figures such as John Dewey and C.S. Lewis and Martin Buber and Martin Luther King. It was just a wonderful experience.

From the very first moment in that seminar together, I knew that we had something that was beyond what people call "chemistry." We had magic. We stimulated each other, we bounced ideas off each other. Cornel would say things that would make me deepen my thinking. I would say things that he says stimulated his thinking. And we were interacting with our students. Pretty soon I couldn't wait for Wednesday to come along, so that we would be back in the classroom together. Those three hours in the evening would go flying by because it was such a wonderful, exhilarating experience. I learned so much just from teaching with him. He's a master teacher.

Out of that experience grew a deep friendship. As Cornel says, "It's beyond a friendship; we're family." He knows my beloved parents. I knew his beloved mother and his daughter Zeytun. She calls me Uncle Robby. I refer to her as my niece Zeytun. It's a very, very deep special relationship, which has been one of the great blessings of my life, not just as a scholar, but as a human being.

Cornel West: Robby is a truth teller in a lot of different ways, and he told the truth there. There's no doubt that he's been a genuine blessing in my life. When I first met Robby, he struck me as one of the few persons who had that paradoxical feature of a serious mind, which is to say, a genuine interest in the perennial issues of what it means to be human, alongside a sense of history: You can already see the one in the many. You can already see that this transcends time, that which is on the one hand, perennial, and on the other hand, contingent and variable and changing. And what that does is it generates a synoptic vision. Robby has a synecdochic imagination, which relates parts to wholes and ways in which the whole is always more than sum of the parts. That's very rare in the highly professionalized, commodified, corporatized academy.

Early on, when they asked me who I would like to talk to, I said, "I'd like to talk to this brother because we never had a chance to spend a sustained amount of time together." Now, we were with towering figures like the radical political philosopher Sheldon Wolin and the liberal political thinker George Kateb and others, so we had a deep appreciation of what intellectual greatness was. And that goes all the way back to the tradition as a whole. I think one of the things we discovered in our conversations and our teachings is that as truth seekers and persons concerned about the perennials of truth and goodness and beauty in the whole and goodness connected to justice, we had to reinforce our calling to keep alive the best of the West.

There's a wonderful line in T.S. Eliot's lovely essay on the British idealist philosopher F.H. Bradley where he says that things are so dim and so grim that it's not even a matter of talking about victory. It's a matter of trying to keep alive the memory of what *arete*, excellence, once was. I think both of us had a sense of living at a particular historical moment and in a culture that was losing access not just to the best of what had gone into the making of it, but more importantly in it—as if you could be indifferent toward it, as if you could be indifferent toward the best and it would have no consequences in the quality of our lives, as well as others around the world.

Now, we always acknowledge the best of other civilizations, empires, and cultures in Asia and Africa, Indigenous peoples, and so forth. But we acknowledged that we had been disproportionately shaped by the West. In our conversations, we always talked about the Socratic legacies of Athens and the Ciceronian legacies of Rome, the prophetic legacies of Jerusalem, the various enlightenments in Europe, as well as the ways in which the underside, the colonialism, the imperialism was always there, no doubt. But at the same time, there were Western voices that were critical of it. So, we talked about Western crimes and about various voices in the West that were critical of Western crimes, so people get a sense of the ambiguous legacies of the various traditions that had shaped us.

Now here he was, a vanilla brother from West Virginia; his grandfathers were coal miners who had been immigrants from Syria and Italy. And here I was, descended from these dignified Africans who were enslaved, from Jim Crow and Jane Crow who were lynched, and so forth. Yet we could come together, wrestling with a sense of what it means to be human, acknowledging that we had been deeply influenced by the best of a series of legacies and traditions.

I mean, if you look at Robby—and both of us in a certain sense—we begin with Plato. But I think Robby goes Plato, Aristotle, and then Cicero and Aquinas, where I begin with Plato, and I probably go to Lucian first, the ancient Greek satirist, and all those other comic writers with their love of incongruity and inconsistency. I'm a passionate lover of Anton Chekhov, and like him, I'm deeply preoccupied with the absurdity and irrationality of human affairs. When we get to modern skeptics like Søren Kierkegaard and Blaise Pascal, we have wonderful fights together. When I first met Robby, I was convinced that Giambattista Vico was the greatest Italian philosopher of all time. Now thanks to Robby, I'm convinced that it's Aquinas, and Vico is a close number two.

But even within this conversation—and we go at it philosophically and theologically—we have these deep commonalities.

And when we get to politics and ideology, people say, "Well, he's supposed to be conservative and you are progressive. He's supposed to be right wing, and you're supposed to be left wing." And we say, "Oh yeah, that is true."

George: We're supposed to be going at it.

West: After all our conversations and times together with our families—and he's going to my daughter's plays, and I'm blessed to spend time with his wife Cindy and his mother and father who are just magnificent exemplars of loveliness and integrity—we say, "Yeah, we're really supposed to be going at each other." And we do have disagreements that in the wider culture can generate very intense polarization. We understand that. There's no doubt about that. There are some very serious things at stake in terms of wrestling with issues like the relation of markets and governments, talking about abortion, and talking about how we understand the ugly legacies of white supremacy and male supremacy and anti-Jewish, anti-Arab, and all ideologies that lose sight of human beings as individuals.

But in the end, what brings us together is something more than a friendship. It is a deep brotherhood. It really is. What brings us together is a fundamental commitment to Socratic intellectual humility. Robby exemplifies it, and he's a masterful teacher of it. Some of the best courses that we've taught, we've had Robby on leftist writers, which I try to accent by teaching on the conservative writers.

One of the things I've tried to do is to make our conversations probably as much about art: Eliot's *Four Quartets*, Franz Kafka's *Metamorphosis*, *Death in Venice* by Thomas Mann, or perhaps the greatest short story in the English language, "The Dead" by James Joyce. And there's Chekhov, of course. I also continually bring out the artistic dimensions of John Coltrane and Beethoven and Chopin and Sarah Vaughan and what have you. And this is one way in which we cross-fertilize each other, at the level of soul, mind, heart. After that you get to civic life, then you get to politics, and these are all inextricably intertwined. You tell me if you agree with that characterization. Does it make sense?

George: Absolutely. The thing that struck me from the beginning—even before we were friends—is that Cornel is a truth seeker. He's got opinions just as I have opinions, he has beliefs and convictions, just as I have beliefs and convictions. But he's the kind of scholar who has not fallen so deeply in love with his opinions that he values them over truth.

A truth seeker is someone who is always willing to subject his opinions, whatever they may be, no matter how deeply held, no matter how cherished, to criticism. Cornel wants to get to the truth of things. Now, because he's a powerful advocate in the public square of the things he believes in, well-known as an activist as well as a scholar, people in general, I think, don't know this about him. It's much clearer if you're in a seminar with him, or when we're driving home together, maybe after an event that we did together late at night. And we're talking about some of these issues. There, it's very clear that what Cornel is fundamentally interested in is getting at the truth of things, especially when it comes to the deepest and most important questions.

We do talk about substantive political issues: tax policies, social issues, environmental questions, and so forth. But those are a relatively small part of our conversation, only because we've got so much else to talk about. Not just philosophical questions, but matters having to do with literature and art, and especially in those areas, I learn so much from him because he is so much more deeply learned than I am in these areas. So, our relationship has caused me to do more reading, for example, on the works of great Russian writers, Leo Tolstoy, Fyodor Dostoevsky, and even Aleksandr Solzhenitsyn, whom I had read only superficially prior to this relationship.

And of course, Chekhov, Cornel's greatest hero. I'd read the standard plays that any decently educated American student would read, but I did not know Chekhov well until Cornel's near obsession with him caused me to think, "You know what? There's got to be some important stuff here for Cornel to be so focused on it." I checked and, of course, indeed, once I got into it, I can see that Chekhov's got deep insights into the complexities of human nature that go well beyond his obvious ideas about human folly. It explains why Cornel's so interested in him. Cornel mentioned this a moment ago, this very interesting difference in intellectual approach that we have where I go from Plato to Aristotle to Aquinas and figures like that.

How does this play out in practice?

George: In the heat of debate, Cornel would see me as being just too rationalist. He would see me as thinking the world is more ordered and therefore more intelligible to the inquiring human intellect than it actually is. In the heat of the same debate, I would perceive Cornel as being too fideist. That means supposing that the disorder of the world is so profound and so innate, we are required, more often than not, at the end of the day, to make leaps of faith about what we cannot actually know by the working of the intellect.

So, where I resonate with an Aristotelian writer like Aquinas, he resonates with a paradoxical thinker like Kierkegaard. He's struck by the absurdity of things in the world. I'm more struck by the order. Now, once we cool down, I realize that Cornel perceives sufficient order in the world to affirm that there are truths that are knowable and that it should be our business, because it's our responsibility, to know them. We can never know them perfectly, we can never know them fully, but we must know them as well as we can to understand the order of the universe—whether it's the moral order, the natural order, the social order, or the supernatural order—we must know them, understand them as deeply as we can. And in that same cool light, Cornel will notice that while I believe that the universe is ordered in a way that renders it fundamentally intelligible to the inquiring human intellect, it is not so tightly ordered that there are no paradoxes or even absurdities.

So, it's more of a difference in emphasis, a difference in what actually strikes us as the most interesting feature of the cosmos. It's parallel in a certain sense to what they sometimes say about Samuel Johnson and James Boswell. It is sometimes said that the difference between Boswell and Johnson—and you see it right there in Boswell's famous biography of his great friend—is that what fundamentally interests Boswell is what's different about people, and what fundamentally interests Johnson is what is the same about people—the common human nature, as opposed to the contingent differences, despite the fact that we're all made out of the same stuff and we're all rational animals, to use Aristotle's phrase.

There's a similar sort of difference in temperament, sensibility, in what strikes us. And because we have that difference, we enrich each other and push each other. It's exhilarating for both of us, and it creates this bond of affection between us. I mean, how can you not love someone from whom you learn in every conversation?

Cornel, do you want to persuade Robby?

West: He's a truth seeker. He's interested in being engaged.

George: It never occurs to me to think in terms of persuading Cornel. I just don't think that. I mean, sure, if I believe something and he doesn't believe it, since I think it's right, I think he'd be better off believing it. So, I certainly want to give him my reasons.

West: Right.

George: But I guess when you respect another person as a genuine truth seeker and recognize that he is as determined a truth seeker as I am, even someone I admire, then when we engage, it's not with a view to persuading him, it's with a view to trying to get to the truth of the thing.

So, you're not trying to change each other's minds?

George: I mean, that's not an operational objective. It could be a consequence. That's true. There's no doubt about that. But we're trying to get at the truth of these things. I mean, I assume if he disagrees with me about something, there's got to be a pretty good chance I'm wrong about it.

West: And I could be wrong, too.

George: He could be wrong, too.

West: Absolutely.

George: So, I put it on the table—or he wants to put it on the table for me—and then we kick it around and see if we can get at the truth of the matter. When you're in this kind of relationship, it's like you're operating as a unit. It's not like there's him and there's me. My job is not to get him to agree with me. We're a unit and we're operating dialectically; he's giving reasons on one side while I'm giving counterarguments on the other side. We're trying to get at the truth. And I know that's his goal. I know his goal is not ideological or to persuade me over to his side. And he knows my goal isn't ideological or to get him on my side. We're not in the business of ideology.

I know that the best way the two of us can get at the truth of things is to get some time together, pour me a nice red Bordeaux, pour him a nice glass of cognac, and let's get to work on trying to figure this thing out. It really doesn't bother me that we don't reach an agreement or that he doesn't come over to my side. I know it doesn't bother him that we don't reach an agreement and I don't come over to his side. We're just trying to get at the truth of things.

Chapter Two

What Is Truth? Why Seek It?

What is truth? Obviously, we understand the difference between a true and a false statement. We understand the distinction between a true and a false theory or proposition. But what is this concept of truth? Where does it come from? What do we mean by that word?

Robert P. George: Human beings by nature desire to be in touch with reality. Now, that desire will sometimes come into conflict with other desires. Sometimes, we'll want things to be true that aren't, and our desire for them to be true will deflect us from the truth. Sometimes, our desire for the truth is overwhelmed by some other passion. The fact that we have a natural human desire to be in touch with reality doesn't mean we will be faithful truth seekers. I don't think anyone in this vale of tears can be a perfect truth seeker because we all have those countervailing or competing desires or temptations. Fallen creatures that we are, we know that sometimes we yield to them. But we shouldn't. We should do everything we can to build a character that will prioritize truth, being actually in touch with reality. Now, that natural human desire, fortunately, is accompanied by a faculty or power, what we call the intellect, which is a truth-attaining faculty.

We can know things by inquiry and deliberation, by grasping the truth of the matter, by judging soundly. Aristotle taught that there are two categories of truth—practical and theoretical—but there's only one intellect. It operates in two ways depending on the category (or type) of truth that we're seeking. But there's a single intellect that experiences, understands, and judges in the domain of practical truth, exercising what Aristotle calls practical reason. Although, remember, there's one and only one intellect, not two different ones. When we're in the domain of practical reason, what we want to know is what is to be done, including what should be done (or not done). We're trying to grasp reasons for action, reasons we should do this, reasons we should not do that, reasons, which, in some cases, are not conclusive. We may have a reason to do X, but we may also have a competing reason not to do X, and there may be no conclusive reason that controls the situation one way or another. It's perfectly morally legitimate to do that, but it's also perfectly morally legitimate not to do that. It would be perfectly morally legitimate for us to go out to dinner tonight, but it would be perfectly morally legitimate for us to forgo that to see a movie or read a book or do something else.

Sometimes, there will be conclusive reasons. Sometimes there will be moral norms that provide conclusive reasons for doing this or for not doing that. These are the "thou shalts" and "thou shalt nots." Then, the other category is what Aristotle called theoretical truth. When we're exercising our theoretical reason, we're trying to figure out not what is to be done or what should be done. We're trying to figure out what is the case about, say, the natural world. This would be the sciences—physics, biology, chemistry, and so forth—or the social world, which we study in economics, political science, sociology, anthropology, or the supernatural world, what we study in theology. The theoretical intellect aims to grasp the truths to get us in touch with reality, about intelligible realities that are out there over against us.

We come out of an Enlightenment tradition where competing truth claims can be allowed to coexist as long as these differences are not worth killing each other over. And yet people once felt very intensely that they were. So, a new order was devised in which truth claims are subject to testing and challenge. That's a very important mechanism, because when people are possessed with a conviction of truth, a certain righteousness can take hold and they will compel you to agree. Is this always going to be a problem?

Cornel West: Whitehead says that Western philosophy is a series of footnotes to Plato. Part of what he means is that if it's Socrates versus the sophist Thrasymachus, who says that might makes right and power dictates truth talk and morals talk, then the younger generation looks to Socrates and asks if this is the case. Can Socrates make an argument about intellectual integrity, rational persuasion, and persuasive argument vis-à-vis what Thrasymachus is putting forward?

When we look at the world, it looks like Thrasymachus certainly has a point. The German philosopher Georg Wilhelm Friedrich Hegel says that history is a slaughterhouse. The British essayist and historian, Edward Gibbon, says it's a series of crimes and follies. Thrasymachus has a lot of evidence here. I think what Brother Robby is alluding to in terms of the inescapability, fragility, and—we hope—desirability of truth-seeking are these flickering candles in the dark—that's really what rational voices, prophetic voices, loving voices, service-oriented voices really are in the history of our species.

For me, anytime you ask, "What is truth?" the greatest text for me in the last hundred years was written by my teacher, the philosopher Hans-Georg Gadamer, *Truth and Method*. He begins with how we are historical, temporal, specific creatures in history and in language. All of us emerge with various traditions. So, in that sense, we're all Gadamerians because we acknowledge we come out of our mothers' wombs, we interact with various persons, and we're socialized into various traditions. It's not just one tradition: it's a variety of different traditions because every tradition is a hybrid anyway, borrowing from what came before and forever growing. The question becomes how do you create what Socrates does vis-à-vis Thrasymachus? How do you create spaces of reason that become zones of persuasion in light of the various traditions we have? The backdrop of those traditions are what? War. Power. Domination. We understand the challenge Thrasymachus represents. We don't accept the conclusion. But we understand the challenge.

So, the issue of traditions becomes what? Always pluralized traditions. How do we adjudicate the various claims made within and across traditions to sustain this Socratic zone of rational persuasion, argument going beyond just power, beyond just conquest? For me, there are three inescapable realities that every human being has to come to terms with: death, dogma, and domination. We all got to die. That's a serious question. Physical death and psychic death. There's social death, civic death, and so forth. There's dogma: religious dogma, ideological dogma, secular dogma, and so forth. Then there's structures of domination. We don't know a moment in the history of the species where all three have not operated. Given that reality, how do you create this Socratic zone of rational persuasion?

Now, by rational persuasion, I don't want to tilt too much in Brother Robby's direction.

George: I was just about to claim that you were!

West: I believe in story and narrative and paradoxical formulation and tragicomic portraits. There are a lot of ways in which we human beings try to create these zones where power and domination and coercion don't completely suffocate us. How do you cultivate desire in the face of death? That's where *paideia* comes in, that is education—deep critical (and self-critical) inquiry and reflection. How do you generate possibilities of dialogue in the face of dogma? That's critical engagement. All these are very feeble and fragile in the history of the species. The third is, how do you render various forms of hierarchy accountable? And that's democracy in the face of domination, not democracy tied to just one particular system, but a system of answerability and accountability in the face of domination that says: "We don't have to account for our power. We just forward our commands and you obey."

In that context, you ask, "Well, where does truth talk come in?" It's within these various traditions that are trying to get us outside of ourselves and make claims about reality, because reality is bigger than our egos. It's bigger than our subjectivities. It's bigger than our families. It's bigger than our tribes. It's bigger than our nations. I would argue that, very much like virtues and the unity of virtues, be they pagan or Christian or Judaic or whatever, that truth is inseparable from beauty and goodness and even the holy. Truth talk without beauty talk is impoverishing to me. Truth, in a way, is like Kierkegaard on love—one and many!

So, truth, then, is a property of reality?

West: There are transcendental universals that get us outside of our egocentric predicament, always in the context of our tradition, because we're temporary historical creatures. However, they're trying to lure us in a direction that takes us beyond coercion, beyond domination, beyond narrow dogma, and beyond death and closure. So, there are ways to pursue the incomplete, unfinished, and endless perennial quest for something bigger than ourselves. It's one end of many. There's a lot of different kinds of truth. There's the truth of the physicist. That's very different from existential truth. There's the truth of the social scientists. That's very different from the truth of the playwright.

Let's look at the seventeenth-century thinker René Descartes. Descartes was a supreme rationalist obsessed with a certain model of knowledge that is tied to clear and distinct ideas. He didn't like opacity. He didn't like the vague, he didn't like the indeterminate. So, what did he do with it? He pushed it aside. He suppressed it. But, hey René, the world's not like that. We got nothing against clear and distinct ideas, but you got a lot of other stuff over here that's not going to be made clear ever. You see what I mean? You go to your mama's funeral, it's not going to be clear and distinct ideas. Something else is going to be going on. And there's truth with her in that coffin. René, what about existential truth? He didn't have too much to say. He didn't have the kind of jazz-like sensibilities to be able to say that maybe actually there are a number of different authorities here.

Maybe we shouldn't go to the Bible if we really want to understand what the relation of sun and earth is, but we could still go there for other deep formulations. Maybe we shouldn't go to physics if we're looking for existential truths. Maybe there's a variety of authorities here. You don't have to have one authority that pushes out all the others. It becomes dogmatic even though it's critical because it's over against what's prevailing at the time. I mean, in Descartes's time, it was Aristotle who was still the great figure when it came to the sciences. He was a scientist in a serious way, but not a modern scientist. And so modern physics had to displace him and come in with mathematization of knowledge, the quantitative models of knowledge, and so forth, for the new physics. It generated unbelievable success, a catastrophe of success. Francis Bacon, Sir Isaac Newton—what do you have to say about Aristotle? "Well, Aristotle's got to go. This old qualitative model's not working anymore. We got mathematical models."

Thank God for John Keats who says, "Beauty is truth, truth beauty." Thank you, John. What are you talking about? He was not talking about electronics. He was not talking about natural objects. He was talking about something else. I think what Keats was talking about was that for him to live in the midst of nineteenth-century modern Europe, with his rich notion of negative capability, meant being in the midst of mystery and doubts and uncertainties without any irritable reaching after fact or reason that he could not find certainty, he could not find foundations, he couldn't find bases or pillars. The only thing that was left dangling for him because he rejected Newton and he rejected Christianity was human relationship. What's left, John? He was a young brother, too. He was going to be dead at twenty-five. So, you aren't going to get an old man's wisdom here. What's left, John? His relationship with Fannie. What's left, John? His relationship to Homer. What's left, John? His intimate relationship with William Shakespeare. That's what sustained him. The beauty of love, the beauty of language, the beauty of art, that he says is the truth of his life. And there's something to that, just as there's something about the truth of the physicist, just as there's something about the truth of Hebrew scripture.

And, of course, for me as a Christian, Jesus is the fleshification of truth. He says, "I am the truth." It's not a proposition tied to states of affairs. It's not words about the world. "I am the truth." What do you mean, Jesus? You're a rabbi. You came out of prophetic Judaism. God is a fleshified person, and it takes a different kind of discourse of truth. It's not correspondence. It's not coherence. In some ways, it's what the German philosopher Martin Heidegger talks about. The truth is *aletheia*. It's revealment and concealment. There's revelation and that which is not revealed and is still hidden. And so, again, truth is many things, but crucially it is *contra* all forms of relativism, *contra* not all forms of skepticism—but of wholesale skepticism.

Skepticism is a good thing. There are deep truths in skepticism because it generates criticism if it's retail skepticism. If it's wholesale then everything's called into question. You can't even begin to think or live. Everything is called into question. So, that skepticism plays its role. The American pragmatist thinker John Dewey, among others, played an important role in making that crucial distinction between different kinds of skepticism tied to different kinds of criticism, tied to pursuing a quest for truth, beauty, goodness, and the holy. I know I've gone on much too long, but I do think truth talk is inseparable from the holy, too. Once you lose that connection of all of them, then you get compartmentalized and specialized fears where people fall between the cracks—meaning, value, beauty, qualitative relations, all of those things fall through the cracks. We live in a cracked-up, messed-up culture where these things are just completely isolated and some are viewed as simply illusions. All truth is thought to be illusion. Beauty is regarded as an illusion. Goodness is an illusion. Justice is an illusion. The holy is an illusion. Well, what's left? Me. My ego. What works for me, how I feel, how I desire. That's a form of spiritual decadence that it would take much longer to try to unpack.

Allan Bloom argued in The Closing of the American Mind *that truth had been relativized, and consequently young people no longer believed in truth. They were cynical about it, with a sense that, well, we've seen through all of that, and all these truth claims have no validity. Now it's thirty years later and it seems we're on the other side of that, and young people now come with dogmatic beliefs, righteous commitment to the truth. How did that happen?*

West: Do you remember Lawrence Levine's response to Allan Bloom, *The Opening of the American Mind?* It is a fascinating dialogue between two very, very crucial figures in the last sixty years. Bloom's argument was, as you recall, that there was a kind of pseudo-Nietzscheanism. There was not a genuine encounter with the genius of the great German philosopher Friedrich Nietzsche. It was a dumbed-down version of Nietzsche, of "anything goes" of no serious attempt to recuperate and recover the best of the West and engage in the deep crisis that the authority of science was presenting to religious people. Now, these are very complicated issues that Nietzsche was wrestling with. The young people were not gaining access to that level of engagement with Nietzsche; they were getting the dumbed-down versions of it. In those versions, they were, ironically, thinking that they were critics of the market when they were actually following market forces.

So, unfortunately, democratization was going hand in hand with commodification so that the students, for example, were coming in saying, "Well, we no longer respect your authority." You say, "Well, where's the authority going to go?" "To us." I said, "Oh, so now we have students as consumers. Is that not a market model? I thought you were critical of the consequences of an unregulated market. Now it's like going into a grocery store and you choose whatever you want, and you want something to make you feel good. Well, I'm sorry, Shakespeare's not going to make you feel good. Dante's not going to make you feel good. Any of the great minds are not going to make you feel good, and we haven't even gotten to Socrates and Jesus yet. The cross is not going to make you feel good."

It was an attempt to first understand what Bloom was saying, which was truth, but the truths were not truths that could fully encompass all the phenomena that was going on. It's what Whitehead used to call "one-eyed reason." There are one-eyed critiques. A critique can tell certain truths but miss out on others. That Bloom was telling certain truths, there's no doubt about it. But at the same time, he was also missing out on some other truths because there were other forces at work that were engaged in some serious critiques of forms of hierarchy and domination, and people were coming out of the twentieth century with fascism, with Stalinism and Nazism and European colonialism and imperialism. Those were real crimes that had consequences on people's perceptions of the world.

Then we jump now to our period where you've had the neoliberals in the driver's seat, so that all the talk about diversity and equity and inclusion become so dumbed down and so leveled that is just a matter of some kind of group, what Brother Robby calls groupthink, narrow dogmatism, feeling good within the group rather than acknowledging how traditions should enable us to think critically for ourselves in relation to forms of suffering that cut across race and gender and national identities and so forth. That has its own grimness and dimness as well. It is just that the neoliberal version becomes even more dangerous in some ways because it's self-righteous.

George: This is always the problem with critique. When you challenge the orthodoxy, you vaunt your intellectual prowess, you've seen through that, and then you offer your own orthodoxy and it becomes just as rigid.

Is this just human nature?

George: Oh, sure. It's human nature.

West: That's true.

George: But that doesn't mean that we need to yield to it.

West: Yeah. It has to be called into question every generation over and over and over and over again.

George: And it's not necessary that critique generates a new form of dogmatism. That's a contingent fact. It's a very common one, but nevertheless, a contingent one.

You might say it's a temptation?

George: It's a constant temptation.

West: Absolutely.

George: And the intellectually and morally and spiritually serious person will know it's a temptation and struggle to resist it, in part by making sure that he's not in an echo chamber, that he is engaging people who will challenge him, that he's learning to challenge himself and be his own best critic.

One problem that I think is perennial is the problem of the vacuum. The ascendancy in our own generation of a kind of almost mindless, certainly uncritical, unsophisticated moral relativism: the idea that there is no truth. That ascendancy created a vacuum, and into that vacuum stepped a rigid dogmatism of the sort that we now find way too common among our students, among young faculty members and intellectuals, and more broadly in the elite sectors of the culture. It's fiercer in some ways than the dogmatism that generated the skeptical critique that brought about the ascendancy of naïve moral relativism for our generation.

Cornel and I—and other people in the academy—find ourselves wrestling today with two challenges to actually educating our students. The first is careerism and ambition, and the reduction of education to a purely instrumental thing—the instrumentalization of education, which goes along with the marketization and commodification of education, the consumer model of education. Students are here to get the classy degree, to acquire the information and skills they need for professional success, career advancement, more money, influence, status, power, prestige. That's challenge number one. Challenge number two is the mindless knee-jerk hostility to everything that has gone before. The belief that institutions and people, because of the sins and injustices of the past, have nothing to teach us.

This is the French revolutionary spirit, that we are the first truly virtuous generation, the first generation that is free of prejudice and hatred and bigotry. So, there's nothing to be learned from Plato or Aristotle, or from Eliot, or in some cases, even from Martin Luther King. King is lionized today in many circles, but there are some people for whom even King is not good enough. Cornel was telling the story of objections he's encountered to his teaching W.E.B. Du Bois, not from people on the right but from people on the left, because Du Bois wasn't woke. He didn't have the right attitudes toward relations between men and women. This is the challenge that we face, and all we can do is encourage the students to adopt a self-critical spirit.

On the one side, it's important for them to understand that there are truths. They can be known and they should be sought. There's a value to pursuing them. On the other hand, we need students to understand that we can never know the truth perfectly, we can never know the whole truth. What we grasp, we will see through a glass darkly, not perfectly, at least in this life. And that because of our own fallibility, indeed fallenness, we are always subject to error.

We can believe we've arrived at the truth, believe it fervently, believe that we've arrived at the most important truths, and yet, be wrong about it. That means that we really can become, in the words of the Yom Kippur liturgy, zealots for bad causes. On Yom Kippur, we—the congregation—beat our breasts and collectively go through our sins: We have stolen, we have cheated, we have lied, we have committed adultery, we have borne false witness, we have been zealots for bad causes.

Now as I often point out, you can't tell a lie accidentally. If you think you're saying something true that happens to be false, it's a falsehood but not a lie. I don't think you can cheat your neighbor accidentally. I don't think you can commit adultery accidentally. It's always something you deliberately did. But whoever deliberately became a zealot for a bad cause? They became zealots for the cause precisely because they thought it was a good cause. But in its great wisdom, the Jewish tradition captures the truth that we can be falsely convinced that our cause is a good one when in fact it's a bad one. That means we always need intellectual humility, we always need a sense of our own fallibility, to genuinely and not merely notionally appreciate our own fallibility.

When we do that, we will never be tyrants because when we recognize our own fallibility, we will always recognize that maybe we have something to learn from the other guy. He might be right and we might be wrong, or he might be at least partially right and we might be partially wrong. Or even if he's entirely wrong and we're entirely right, at least if he's a thoughtful person, engaging with him to understand how he ended up where he did can deepen and enrich our understanding of the topic. Here I'm simply rehearsing points that were made by the nineteenth-century philosopher John Stuart Mill in chapter two of his great work *On Liberty*. We will not, if we have a keen sense of our own fallibility, if we have the intellectual humility Cornel and I try to exemplify in our own imperfect ways, but certainly preach to our students, you won't try to shut down an interlocutor, you will not become an enemy of free speech. And you'll listen to other people who want to challenge you. You will not treat your conversation partner, however much you disagree and however important the question is, as an enemy to be defeated. You'll treat him as a friend with whom you're in partnership, a dialectical partnership maybe, but nevertheless a partnership in the cause of trying to get at the truth of things.

There's an apparent distinction between a truth teller and a truth seeker, which is that the truth teller makes a claim to possess the truth. There are certainly truths that someone can utter that will get them in trouble. But the truth seeker is challenging or unsettling in a different way. Which is riskier? To be a truth teller or a truth seeker?

George: I don't think you can separate them. If you have a putative truth teller who is not a truth seeker, you don't have a truth teller, you have an ideologue or a dogmatist. Ultimately, to be a truth teller, you have to first be a genuine truth seeker. And if you're a genuine truth seeker, that means you can never be an ideologue or a dogmatist. You'll never be someone caught up in groupthink and intellectual conformism.

West: That's true. But keep in mind what Rainer Maria Rilke says in *Letters to a Young Poet*—that it's not just a question of raising the questions, but living the questions. The reason Socrates is what he is, is not just because he raised questions, but because he lived them. He exemplified the spirit of critique existentially.

George: As a way of life.

West: As a way of life. And he was willing to pay whatever cost and bear the consequences that went along with pursuing the questions. In that sense, Brother Robby's absolutely right in terms of a truth teller. But truth tellers usually have to be measured by the degree to which they're willing to tell painful truths about themselves, and then tell painful truths about the group from which they come. When I hear young people say, "I'm speaking truth to power," I say, okay, all right, settle down, let's relax now. These are rhetorical gestures and spectacles at times—okay, fine—but nobody's going to jail. So, let's just be honest about this.

But when you start pursuing questions seriously and say, "Well, I'm a feminist. I believe in women's dignity, humanity, and so forth." Okay. But then I ask if, as a woman, are you willing to speak painful truths to other women? As a Black person, am I willing to speak painful truths to Black people? Or anybody? Jewish people, conservatives, whoever. All the ugliness and the civil war taking place in the soul of each and every one of us. So, that's truth-telling tied to truth-seeking. Because truth-seeking is that capital-T truth. You're never going to get to it. You're a finite person. All of us are failed, cracked vessels in that sense, I think.

As teachers you have had an opportunity to observe young people up close for many years. Do you find that young people today still have an appetite for knowledge? What kind of students do you attract?

George: There's no question that a certain number of students want to be in our classes because we're both well known, especially Cornel, who is a very well-known celebrity professor. But we can only have eighteen students in a seminar; if you expand it beyond that number, it will turn into a lecture course and the magic will be gone. Since we're restricted to eighteen, what happens is several hundred students will want to sign up and then we have to decide how we are going to choose. Now, some professors make choices like that by having students submit essays explaining why they would like to be in the course. There are some pros to that, but there are some cons as well. So, we decided that we would just have a random selection of students.

Some students are there because the professors are well known and they're known to have this interesting relationship. But I would say most of our students are there because they're interested in the questions of meaning and value that we put in the forefront, and they don't have enough opportunities to explore those questions across the curriculum. Even in courses where, for example, Plato or Aristotle are read, very often the course is devoted to commentaries, a lot of reliance on secondary sources. Questions of what do scholars think about the translation of this word or that word, devolving into technical discussions—not always, but very often. And there's a place for that. Those can be good courses too, but there should also be courses like ours. We assign no secondary readings. In fact, we tell students, "We can't police this, but please, we ask you not to read commentaries. Now, later, we will recommend to you the commentaries that we ourselves think are the best ones. But please don't read them now. We want you to engage the author directly." Now we realize there are translation issues and things like that, but the goal is to wrestle with the questions the authors are wrestling with. We're going to treat the authors as our conversation partners.

This is not a seminar about the interpretation of Plato, or the interpretation of the *Apology*, or the interpretation of Aristotle. This is a course where we, in conversation with each other, with the students, and with Plato or Aristotle, are going to address the great questions of meaning and value that they wrestled with. That's what we're about. And there's a market for that. Students are interested in it, but they've got to be encouraged. Sometimes they have to be provoked. Sometimes you have to do a little of the crowbar operation of opening their minds because they come in with a head stuffed with ideology. It might be left-wing, it might be right-wing, it might be religious, it might be secular—but their head is so stuffed with dogma that you need to open it up so they'll really wrestle with the questions and begin thinking for themselves.

West: That's right. With our students, I think there's a push and a pull. I think on the one hand, Robby has a reputation of trying to uphold the intellectual standards of the West, not just as a philosopher, but as something that's almost prudence, connected to juris. It's not the narrow, legalistic, positivistic understanding, it's the tradition of *phronesis*, or what today we would call prudence or practical judgment as it relates to institutions of law and religion. That's going all the way back to Cicero again. So, Robby introduces them to the Socratic, the Platonic, the Aristotelian, as well as Cicero and natural law theorists like Hugo Grotius and Samuel von Pufendorf. He has also a reputation of being fair so you have a variety of perspectives in the class across ideology, across politics. And then my reputation, whatever it is, when we get together, they figure, "Wow, this should be explosive."

That's partly what they're looking for. And they're surprised because it *is* explosive, but it's *intellectually* explosive. It's substantively explosive. Because we come in talking about death, dread, disappointment, disenchantment, and how do you deal with nihilism and skepticism and cynicism and fatalism. All of a sudden, many of them may say, "Well, we might not know exactly what these words mean, but we've had moments of meaninglessness and hopelessness and touchlessness and love-lessness." You don't say! Join the human club. That's what it is to wrestle with what it means to be human. And so, there is that kind of intellectual explosion that they get.

I think you remember that moment we had though, brother, when we were talking about the great Matthew Arnold, and nobody had read him. And I said, "Robby, I think it's time to cry, brother. It's time to shed some tears, man." You remember when we went around the room, remember that?

George: It was actually even worse than that.

West: Was it?

George: So, we decided for one of our seminars that we would assign among the readings, John Henry Newman's work *The Idea of a University.* The book is a collection of lectures Newman had given in the 1850s arguing that knowledge should be pursued for its own sake. But by this he did not mean pure research. For him the search for truth was something that shaped the personality of the cultivated individual, and was inseparable from moral and religious education. It was an important book for both of us in our own intellectual journeys, and we thought it would be good to have it in the mix of books we were getting the students to talk about, since it focused on what the students were there to do, namely, to get a liberal arts education. What does it mean to be liberally educated? What does it mean to be appropriating the richness, the wealth of traditions of thought by way of a university education? We assigned it as an experiment. We didn't know if it would work because Newman's language is very baroque and his vision is one that's quite different in important ways from what passes as liberal arts education today.

West: Oh, absolutely.

George: So, we didn't know whether the students would resonate with it. I didn't expect that they would. I thought they might find it just alien and unhelpful. My hope was that at least it would be somewhere in the middle and that they would get something out of it. Well, to our astonishment, they resonated with Newman. It was one of the best discussions we've had, and we've had some wonderful discussions. They were rocking and rolling, playing off Newman's idea of what it meant to be enriched by a true liberal arts education.

And it occurred to me, especially since they were so enthusiastic about the book, that in a way the experiment also indicated that they were surprised by the ideas. The ideas struck them as new. It occurred to me to ask the question, "How many of you (I put the standard very low) have heard of (I didn't ask if they'd actually read) John Henry Newman, before entering this class and being assigned this book?" I expected that not everybody would have heard of Newman, otherwise I wouldn't have asked the question. But I also expected at least the Catholic kids—and Catholic students are about 20 percent of the population at a place like Princeton—would have at least heard of him. But not a single student raised a hand. Not a single student, including the Catholic students, had even heard of, much less read anything by Newman.

So, I looked at Cornel. Cornel looked at me. And we vocalized our thoughts, which I think now in retrospect we shouldn't have done, because I think the students took it the wrong way. We looked at each other and almost in unison said, "This isn't their fault. This is our fault. This is the fault of educators." If these young men and women have not even heard of, much less read, a figure as important to what they're doing at a place like Princeton as Newman, they can't be blamed. We at the professorial level are responsible for them not knowing this.

But then I went on and talked about other nineteenth-century English writers. "I know you've heard of Matthew Arnold, John Ruskin, William Morris"—but then I stopped, "Well, let's just take Matthew Arnold. How many of you have heard of Matthew Arnold?"

West: And I said, "Oh my God."

George: One girl half-raised a hand, only half. And she said, "I think I have." And I said, "Oh, that's good. At least you think you have." And then I asked, "What are you majoring in?" And she said—I'm not making this up—English literature.

West: It was like, "Oh my God, this is a moment for weeping, but we're weeping for you as you undergo your awakening."

George: And then Cornel gave them a little lecture. He said, "There's a library there. Even if your professors are not assigning these writers, you should be inquiring who are the best thinkers of the past, who are the best writers of the past, and then go to that library and get the books and read them yourself. You have some responsibility here too in your education. Yes, your professors have let their side down in some important ways, but you have a responsibility on your own."

West: And the good news is, there was a student who did come to me two or three years later and talked about Arnold. He said he remembered that moment. So, I asked him, "Well, did you follow through?" He said he had. And so, I bought him an old version of Lionel Trilling's dissertation on Arnold, the magisterial book he published at Columbia in 1939. And I said, this is Arnold and company. You're going to get a whole conception of what the best of the West is, as understood by this particular brother in the 1930s. And so that hunger and that thirst does come through if you provide exposure, encouragement, and some critical engagement. And that's good news.

George: To go back to a point we touched on earlier, I want to be clear that to be a truth seeker and a truth teller, one needn't lead the life of Socrates. He had a particular vocation.

West: Right. That's true.

George: You can be a used car salesman.

West: Absolutely.

George: An investment banker, a housewife, a professor, an editor, an insurance executive, and be a truth seeker and a truth teller. It's not something that stands alongside all these other things. Anybody, in any walk of life can and should be a truth seeker and a truth teller, even if scholarship is not your vocation, even if activism of some sort is not your vocation. Your vocation may be medicine. You can still be, you need to be a truth seeker and a truth teller.

West: Keep in mind, that's very Emersonian, very American of Robby because there are traditions that would confine truth tellers and truth seekers to a small, small group of elites at the top. Very much so. Even Plato wouldn't agree with you on that. Aristotle wouldn't agree with you on that. Robby's been Emersonianized and Americanized, but it has its roots in Hebrew scripture and the—

George: I think it reflects my Christian biblical vision more than it does Emerson.

West: But would Augustine and Aquinas agree with you in terms of a janitor having the capacity for truth-telling the same way a priest would?

George: Yeah, I think they would.

West: I don't know about that. Your language about this is the kind of democratization that's there in the scriptures, but at that time it remained latent and implicit, especially when it came to church structures and intellectuals and scholars tied to the church.

George: What's striking is that human institutions, including church structures, can always go wrong in various ways, fall short, need to be reformed, and so forth. But I'm sure that figures like Augustine or Aquinas would understand that among the things that parents do for their children, among the things that a mother does for—

West: Like Augustine's mother, St. Monica, who famously encouraged his search for the truth of Christian beliefs.

George: That's right—from the very beginning parents encourage, empower, and impart the virtues necessary for children to be formed as truth seekers and truth tellers.

Chapter Three

From the Age of Feeling to the Joy of Thinking

You've both spoken and written about the heritage of Athens and Jerusalem that runs through Western civilization and gives it its special dynamism, the tension between reason and faith. They represent two kinds of truth, one might say. Is that the case? Do these traditions each have a valid and competing truth claim?

Robert P. George: Sometimes historians break up the epochs into the age of this and the age of that. For example, sometimes historians refer to the medieval period as the Age of Faith. And while that's an oversimplification, of course, there's some truth to it. For the great medieval thinkers, early, middle, and late, the ultimate touchstone or criterion of not only truth but of virtue, rightness, justice was conformity with the teachings of the faith.

Now, that's not to say that they didn't value reason. Nobody can read the ten thousand questions addressed by Thomas Aquinas in his enormous corpus of work without being powerfully struck by his high view of reason. But still, it is not crazy to think of the medieval period as the Age of Faith.

And people, historians and others, who break up the epochs into the age of this and the age of that will then refer to the Enlightenment as the Age of Reason or the Age of Science. Again, that's an oversimplification, and it neglects that fact that there were many different "Enlightenments," but it does contain some truth. For many "Enlightenment" figures, reason was given a very high place. The touchstone for them of truth and justice and goodness is conformity to reason.

Well, if the medieval period was the Age of Faith and the Enlightenment era was the Age of Reason, what's our age? I think—and fear—that our age is an Age of Feeling. Truth has been reconceived as a matter of feeling, not something to be attained by reason and rational inquiry. This is what generates the absurd and laughable idea of there being "my truth" and "your truth"—as opposed to simply the truth. It's not faith or reason that is regarded today as the touchstone of truth, goodness, rightness, or justice. It's feelings. It's how I subjectively feel about something that characterizes it or determines it to be true or false, or enables us to judge it to be right or wrong, good or bad. And the one thing we know about feelings is they are very unreliable.

I'm not promoting stoicism or Buddhism, although I have great respect for those traditions. I'm not saying we should eliminate or try to extinguish our feelings. But I do think that feeling is an unreliable guide to truth, an unreliable guide to what is in fact right and just. We can be led astray by our feelings. Our reason is fallible, certainly. Having my high view of reason doesn't guarantee that I or anybody else is going to be right all the time or even most of the time. We do our best. But I know that feelings are going to lead us astray an awful lot of the time. That's why I want the touchstones of truth and goodness to be faith and reason not feeling. Now, I'm going to sound very Catholic here because I am a Catholic and to Cornel's ears, I'm going to sound very rationalist.

Cornel West: That's all right, Robby. That's all right.

George: A good Catholic can sound very rationalist to Cornel's Baptist ears. But I agree with Pope John Paul II in his great encyclical *Fides et Ratio* that faith and reason, far from being in conflict or even tension, are mutually supportive and both necessary for a full and rich understanding of the truth—an understanding that we ourselves in this life will never fully achieve, but to which we should aspire. It's our ideal.

He opens that encyclical with a really beautiful image. He says that faith and reason are the two wings on which the human spirit ascends to contemplation of the truth. They're not exactly the same thing, but neither can do without the other. This is why, at least on the Catholic side of Christianity, it seems so natural and right to appropriate the teachings of the great pagan Greek and Roman philosophers and jurists. So, although some Protestants are scandalized by the way Aristotle's categories and ideas were brought into Christian philosophy and theology, it seems very natural and right to me. Same with Plato and same with Cicero.

My view, which is a sort of small-C Catholic as well as large-C Catholic view, is that we should get at the truth and embrace the truth and bring ourselves into line with the truth wherever we can find it. The Second Vatican Council has a beautiful document called *Nostra aetate*. It is most famous for its teaching on Jews and Judaism, repudiating all forms of anti-Semitism, repudiating the idea that God has rejected the Jewish people or abrogated his covenant with them. And it's profoundly import-ant for that reason. But people who think of it as a document just about Christianity and Judaism haven't read the whole thing because it's actually a document on the church's under-standing of and relationship with all the various non-Christian faiths—Judaism to be sure, but Islam, Buddhism, Hinduism, even the native traditions of various Indigenous peoples in Africa and in North America and elsewhere as well.

The document affirms, from the Catholic vantage point, that there are important truths to be found in these traditions. It says we as Catholics embrace all that is true and holy in all the non-Christian faiths. Not only do we embrace it, but we are willing and should be eager to learn from it and incorporate these truths into our own understanding. It is un-Catholic for a Catholic to suppose that we have nothing to learn from traditions outside the Christian faith. And that's because people have reason and people have formed traditions, which are traditions of wisdom. Christianity is one, but not the only one. And it's not just the biblical faiths of Christianity and Judaism, it's not just the Abrahamic faiths of Christianity and Judaism and Islam. It includes the others, even those that are from our perspective the more primitive faiths. We can learn from them.

Now, of course, as a Catholic, one must believe that Christianity contains the fullness of truth on these matters, although any serious Catholic Christian will also acknowledge that we still don't know everything there is to know. There are still mysteries. There are still unknowns. But the belief is that on the distinctive Christian claims, Christianity has it right.

My point here is simply to emphasize that it's important for a truth seeker to recognize that truth is to be found in many, many, many, many places and in many, many, many different traditions. It's important to embrace truth and bring it into one's life, no matter where it comes from, no matter where you find it.

West: Absolutely.

George: I think the abandonment of the tradition that begins with the Hebrew revelation inevitably sinks back into paganism. Not the virtuous paganism of Plato and Aristotle, but the brutal paganism about which Heinrich Heine warned in 1834. Heine, the German-Jewish Christian poet, published a statement that prophesied what came to pass a hundred years later when Hitler came to power.

Now, he didn't say there would be a guy with a little mustache named Adolf Hitler or a party called the National Socialists or anything like that. What he said was: "Christianity, and this is its greatest merit, has somewhat mitigated the brutal German love of war, but it could not destroy it. Should that subduing talisman, the cross, be shattered, the frenzied madness of the ancient warriors, that insane Berserk rage of which the Nordic bards have spoken and sung so often, will once more burst into flame. This talisman is fragile. And the day will come when it will collapse miserably. Then the ancient stony gods will rise from the forgotten debris and rub the dust of a thousand years from their eyes. And then Thor, with his giant hammer, will jump up and smash the Gothic cathedrals."

He then said, "Don't smile at a man who foresees himself." In other words, at a man who foresees happening in the realm of the visible what has already happened in the realm of the invisible, the realm of the spirit, *geist*. In the realm of thought. Don't smile at someone who predicts that this will come, this evil will come. Just as thunder follows lightning. He said, "A play will be performed in Germany which will make the French Revolution look like an innocent idyll." He saw exactly where things would go if that subduing talisman—if Christianity, for all its faults—would collapse.

I think the same is true of individuals such as the pro-Nazi German philosophers Carl Schmidt and Martin Heidegger. When their faith collapsed, it didn't get replaced with nothing or with some mild-mannered western liberal sort of elixir. It got replaced by exactly what Heine predicted would replace it, what had been there before, but now in a radicalized form.

West: I think what Heine also saw—he's a Jewish brother, converted to Protestantism—he knew that the ideological idol of his day was nationalism. When religious authority collapsed, nationalism, especially German nationalism, was reinforced after World War I with indebtedness, with the marginalization, with the reparations, and with the stripping of the German Empire of all its colonies. That's like castrating the brother at the wrestling match or something. I mean, for Germany to be off the international stage with no more colonies, you might have just cut his privates off in that sense, right? And so, Heidegger was actually making choices with these various options, but it was the deeply nationalistic option that seduced him as it did most Germans.

How did we get to the age of feeling? Does it have something to do with the rise of nineteenth-century Romanticism? And isn't that somehow tied to the rejection of Christianity, of classical virtue, any kind of external constraint? And a kind of falling in love with the old gods?

George: Absolutely right.

West: Or the God of one's own self.

George: Yeah, I mean Jean-Jacques Rousseau, with his idea of the "noble savage," has a lot to answer for. He wasn't alone. In a certain sense, he was just the messenger of the spirit of the age—the loss of the sense of human fallenness and human fallibility, what Christians would call original sin. This leads to the notion that feeling and emotion are a reliable guide and the abandonment of the idea that we need to rely on reason to govern our feelings and emotions.

West: Absolutely.

George: The most important thing about a man is that he feels; that's the truth of who he is. The truth of his feelings is more important than anything else.

West: But you see, part of what we must keep in mind is that all these movements have a sunny side and a dark side. With Romanticism, you do have a denaturalizing and a historicizing of both self and society that generates possibilities of change. If you have a self that's repressing your feelings, then (as Freud said) there's going to be a return of the repressed sooner or later. And when you think of the Romantics, I mean, Wordsworth and Keats and Coleridge are one thing, the Germans are something else, the French are something else, the Spanish are something else. This is very interesting with regard to my dear Brother Robby here. There is no America without the Romantic movement.

George: There's truth in that.

West: Because of its revolutionary aspirations. There's a train of abuses on us now. Now they're talking about the slaves. They're not talking about Indigenous people. They're talking about these folk in these thirteen colonies, and we are going to use our imagination and courage for a fundamental transformation. That's Romantic energy.

George: Well, it's a new human being that was a redeemed human.

West: Well, even the ones who wouldn't go that far. I'm thinking of somebody like Thomas Jefferson. Jefferson would never use the phrase "new human being." He had too much sense of reality in him. But he had revolutionary fervor. Very much so. Part of the challenge is to be able to see what was in place to lead toward this kind of one-sided response that would valorize feeling and subjectivity and community and nation. Because there's no nationalism without Romanticism in the early stages, too. You see what I mean? So, what they were responding to was just, the self was too cold. The neoclassical notions of proportionality and equipoise and calmness and so forth. I mean, is that going too far?

George: No, I think you're onto something. But that raises to my conservative mind the question we sometimes have to ask ourselves: What do we fear the most? Where's the greater danger?

Too much order. Too little order.

George: Yeah, too much order, too little order. And here, even a figure like Martin Luther King would say the most dangerous thing is too little order. Now, that doesn't mean we don't reform the order that we've got when it is askew and wrong.

But the worst thing of all is a kind of lawlessness. An utter disorder, anarchy.

West: That's true. But if you go toward Thomas Hobbes—

George: Then you're at the extreme in the other direction.

West: Exactly. That's his starting point.

Or consider a historical figure like Napoleon, who is a tyrant but who also stimulated liberal revolutions. He inspired the Romantic movement. All those great operas and symphonies.

West: He didn't begin as a tyrant. He became a tyrant. Beethoven was writing the *Eroica* and wanted to dedicate it to Napoleon. But he became a tyrant, an emperor. So, scratch it out, scratch it out. Napoleon generated a certain energy and aspiration because he was going to try to create some kind of legal codes that were more egalitarian.

He also inspired a new kind of heroic individualism: the idea that I, too, can be great, I, too, have a personal destiny.

West: He inspired people to think for themselves.

George: I guess my spirit is more the spirit of Christian humanists like Erasmus and Thomas More. They were under no illusions when it came to corruption in both church and state and the need for reforms and renewal. But unlike Martin

Luther and some others, they did not want reform to turn into a radical fracturing, especially of the church.

West: I thought you were going to say Edmund Burke.

George: Well, yes, Edmund Burke. He's another reformer who insisted that reform must be deliberate, even a bit cautious, lest it unleash evils worse than those the reform was meant to rectify. Read, for example, his reflections on the French Revolution. Incidentally, Cornel's invocation of Burke here demonstrates something I want people to know about my dear brother. He's widely thought of as this great leftist, progressive, even radical figure. But I'm getting the whole reactionary side of him now. You can't find somebody on the conservative side who knows and admires Burke as much as Brother Cornel does. You can't find somebody who understands and appreciates supposed right-wing philosophical reactionaries like Eric Voegelin or Leo Strauss as much as Cornel does. But most people don't know that. I do!

West: Well, I tell them if they ask!

Then tell us. What do you like about Burke?

West: He had a deep grasp of the underside of the French Revolution. He knew where that was going. And while he supported the Americans in their revolution, he could see the difference between the two. He also supported the Irish against the British empire.

George: Exactly.

West: He was an independent thinker who understood the crucial role of tradition. The radical difference between somebody like an Edmund Burke and myself—and here I just follow William Hazlitt and the wonderful work of the critic David Bromwich and others, because Hazlitt loved Burke probably more than any other figure, and he's about as left wing as you can get. But he knew that what Burke was doing was understanding the historical character of who we are as persons. And the inescapability of tradition is just that Burke had a kind of organically incremental and traditionalist understanding of tradition. My understanding of tradition goes back to Jesus. It's a prophetic tradition of resilience and resistance different from a traditionalist understanding of tradition that highlights hierarchical order.

You can have a tradition of resilience and a resistance that acts as justice, but it's still a tradition. And you can't have justice without order. Brother Robby connected it in that way, right? You can't have freedom without some kind of constraint, or you just have licentiousness. You can't have critical thinking without having some kind of conception of the great. Because if all you have to fall back on is Donald Duck and Mickey Mouse, then we're all in a world of trouble.

But we are talking about Plato, Aristotle, Dante, Shakespeare, and Coltrane. We're talking about a whole constellation of figures who, through vocation and tradition, provided us tremendous sources to wrestle with what it means to be human. In that sense, Burke understands that so well. He has a critique of imperialism, but it is an imperial critique of imperialism. But everybody doesn't agree with me. I mean, I am anti-imperialist, but I can still learn a lot from Burke's critique of imperialism in India or his support of the Americans.

George: I do think that any healthy society, whether its form of government is republican or not, will have a politics that includes movements or parties of reform and of conservation. And I think that would capture both the spirit of Burke on the one side and the spirit of Hazlitt or Brother Cornel here on the other side. I don't think you would want a society that only had the spirit of Hazlitt, nor would you want a society that only had the spirit of Burke. It's hard to combine those in an individual, but societies are not individuals. I think what would emerge, your best shot at getting decency to emerge in a society, humane policies, having a rough balance of the elements of reform and the elements of conservation.

West: Absolutely. I mean that's why any conception of tradition has to have an "s." You historicize, you contextualize, you pluralize, but also you have to allow different voices to be heard. We're back to the Black national anthem again, right? You got to allow these voices to be heard. We needed Thomas Paine. Paine's concept of tradition was pretty weak, but we needed his voice. But are you going to put Paine in control of things? No. Tom, you go back up to upstate New York, continue to write your pamphlets. But you also needed some of the more conservative things.

*You need a John Adams, who was appalled by
the French Revolution, while Thomas Jefferson
embraced some of its radicalism.*

West: Exactly. You need an Adams. And you definitely need
later on a Frederick Douglass or Harriet Tubman. You need
these different voices. You're going to need these new immigrants coming from Italy and Ireland and Eastern Europe and
Haiti, Russia, and so forth. They're going to add something
that's going to be very different from what's in place. And it's
going to continue to this very day with new immigrants from
India and Ethiopia and what have you. But they're all human
beings. They're all cracked vessels. You're not going to roman-
ticize any of them, you're not going to idealize any of them.
But they've got much to learn, and we've got much to learn
from them.

*Earlier you used the phrase "self-evident truths." It seems
that young people today are coming into your class who feel
that they are in possession of truths that are not necessarily
compatible with Jefferson's idea of a divine or natural law.*

George: This gets us right back to the Age of Feeling. If your
feelings count as your truth or you let them count, or I allow
them to be counted as your truth, then they are unquestion-
able. There's no conversation to be had. There's nothing to be
learned. But that's the error of putting feelings at the center
of everything and allowing feelings to control where reason is
allowed to function as the standard of judgment. So, feelings

have to be subjected to critical scrutiny. Yes, you feel this way, but *should* you feel this way? That question of *should* you feel this way cannot be answered by asserting a feeling. You need *reasons* why you should feel this way or why you shouldn't feel this way.

West: I think it's important to distinguish between some of the very profound and sophisticated critiques of, for example, the kind of truth talk that Robby and I put forward say, on Nietzsche versus the more pseudo-Nietzschean or juvenile Nietzschean talk about feelings and sophomoric relativism. Nietzsche raises the questions, "What makes us think that truth is a good thing? What is the value of truth itself? What if the fundamental truth about things leads toward self-destruction?"

You get this in Eugene O'Neill's *The Iceman Cometh*, which is one of the greatest Nietzschean critiques of the kind of thing that Robby and I represent. O'Neill is following both August Strindberg, the great Swedish playwright who was his master, and Nietzsche, who was also his master. His argument is that once you awaken people and critically engage the world, and they discover how grim it is, then that truth itself leads toward Harry Hope's saloon—where of course there is no hope. You can only drink yourself to death. No courage. Nobody can walk out, nobody can form qualitative relations with each other. *The Iceman Cometh* is probably one of the most profound plays written in American theater. Young folk need to be exposed to that.

I teach *The Iceman Cometh* in prison just like I teach *Waiting for Godot*, which is a favorite play in prison. We read "The Student," Chekhov's story about truth and beauty connecting all human experience, in prison; we read it out loud with the brothers. Why? Because we've got a lot of time, and because I can expose myself in ways that's a little bit different in the classroom. But that's one critique, and we do have to come to terms with that. Nietzsche is no joke. And every major intellectual has to come to terms with Nietzsche and Schopenhauer and Strindberg and all of those kinds of critiques. That's part of the Socratic conversation.

But when you start invoking your experience as a way of shielding yourself from critique, that's just child's play now. Let's grow up. We need some maturity here. We need some uncertainty and ambiguity. "Well, I want to be in a safe place." No, we make it very clear. This place is a place in which we respect each other, but it is not safe at all. When we finish reading *Antigone*, if you don't feel like stepping off the cliff for a moment, then you haven't read it well. And we haven't gotten to *Hamlet* yet.

George: Cornel says to our students: "If you're looking for a safe space, you're in the wrong classroom." That's how our courses begin.

West: *This is not a safe space.* It's not safe for Robby or me. We're holding on to each other for dear life. Robby, should we get a cognac and wine and the Bible too? Because that's what Shakespeare does to you—*King Lear*, those howls of ultimate despair at the end and so on.

George: That's part of what Cornel said to the students, that "the whole point of the education you're receiving is to unsettle you." Whatever a student's views are—right, left, center, religious, secular—no matter what they are, we're going to unsettle those views. They're all going to be on the table and subjected to critical scrutiny.

West: There are going to be moments in which your worldview rests on pudding. That's called a moment in your educational process.

George: The philosopher Alasdair MacIntyre ends his famous book, *After Virtue*, by saying that the choice before us is really a choice between Nietzsche and Aristotle. And I think there's an awful lot of truth to that. This, I think, is what Cornel is getting at when he says, "Nietzsche is no joke." Nietzsche is the real alternative to the Aristotelian view, the high view of reason and truth. And if we take Nietzsche seriously, believing that there is no final truth and our opinions are founded on nothing, we are back with Thrasymachus in *The Republic* and really facing up to the question of whether might makes right.

West: Nietzsche's complicated. He was in love with Socrates. He was in love with Jesus. But he hated most of the rationalists coming out of Socrates and he hated Christianity coming out of Jesus. The British philosopher and critic John Cowper Powys argued that Nietzsche was an intellectual sadist, which is to say, he used to say being an intellectual is not a matter of having the courage of one's conviction. It's having the courage to attack one's own most precious convictions. And some of Nietzsche's most precious convictions were actually Christian. He came from a generation of Lutheran ministers, and this sense of being associated with the weak and sympathy for the poor, spreading loving kindness and steadfast love, to the orphans and widows and vulnerable—

George: The Jewish tradition.

West: So, the Jewish notion coming out of Hebrew scripture, you see, that Nietzsche first absorbed, and then revolted intensely against, it was still a part of him. So, he ended up attacking viciously some of the most precious things that he held dear, and he snapped. Now people snap for different reasons, but he happened to snap at the moment he was protecting a helpless mule that was being mistreated. Meaning what? Meaning in part that he didn't have that kind of inner tension, that complication and complexity, even though he ended up with might over right and with the will to power—as he dramatically wrestled with overcoming nihilism.

George: Yeah.

West: But with Nietzsche himself, when you look at each step of the process, early Nietzsche, middle Nietzsche, later Nietzsche, *Antichrist* at the end, and then eleven years living with his mama not knowing basically where he was, you say, boy, now that is what it is to take seriously the intellectual vocation even though one has some of the deepest disagreements with him.

Robby, in one of your interviews, you explained why you defend Peter Singer, a utilitarian thinker who justifies positions many consider morally repugnant, because he unsettles you and makes you think. Why do we say that something "made us think"? To me it suggests that thinking is something we don't really want to do. It's challenging and scary. But you two seem to take a real pleasure in thinking. How do you make people think?

George: This is an area where, when we're teaching, the example we try to set is important. Of course, it's important to teach by "precept," too. We have to talk, we have to lecture a bit, maybe even preach a little to the students in our charge. But that's only part of the picture. The most important part is teaching by example. I think the students learn more from seeing us, especially seeing us together, allowing ourselves to be challenged, our most fundamental views to be challenged, allowing that, encouraging that, and at the same time taking joy in it, finding joyful the experience of thinking, the experience of truth-seeking. It's contagious when students see it.

First, they realize they can do it, too. Second, they realize that it takes a certain kind of courage, because when you're thinking critically—self-critically—you really don't know where you're going to end up. If you're a genuine truth seeker, you're putting questions on the table, you're putting your most cherished convictions on the table. You don't know who you're going to be at the end. That can be frightening because we do tend to wrap our emotions more or less tightly around our convictions.

Our sense of identity is bound up with what we believe. But if I'm putting my most fundamental beliefs on the table, genuinely doing that, I don't know whether I might change my mind. I might end up being something or someone different. So, it takes courage to be willing to do it. When young men and women see the courage exemplified, they're much more likely to make the attempt themselves.

And then they see the payoff where we've really deepened our understanding, that we're at a better place at the end of the conversation. Even if we haven't resolved the issue, we're at a better place. We have a deeper grasp of the issues than we did at the beginning. And they can understand the intelligible value of that intellectual progress.

West: That's why I use the phrase "the joy of thinking" rather than "the pleasure of thinking." Because I think our young people, they're living in the most commodified, commercialized, market-driven culture of the species. So much of their culture can be characterized as a joyless quest for insatiable pleasures. So, they get almost any kind of pleasure they want available, a variety of different venues and forms, but end up joyless.

The question then becomes, "What's the difference between joy and pleasure?" Well, you see, thinking requires so much courage to cut against the grain, whereas pleasure so often is associated with going with the grain. It's almost for Christians like ourselves where to be *in* the world, but not *of* the world. That's why joy is a fruit of the love that one has in relation to God.

George: So, you can be "surprised by joy."

West: Just like in C.S. Lewis's wonderful book of that title. But it's a joy because again, it's an interruption of the dominant ways of the world. Even Heidegger with his ugly Nazi self in his book, *What Is Called Thinking?*, says that very few people really want to think. And of course, he's going to Dostoevsky (who hung on his office wall). How many people really want to be free rather than following the Grand Inquisitor with all the turning of mystery into manipulation and magic? How many people really want to think? It costs too much. There's too much risk. You could end up in nihilistic zones. You can end up in a skeptical context. We've talked before about how nihilism and skepticism are always closets in any room of a serious thinker. There's just no doubt about it. And that's why when MacIntyre ends at Nietzsche or Aristotle, he knows that the two are intertwined. It's not going to be just all Aristotle on one side and crushing Nietzsche out, or all Nietzsche on one side and pushing Aristotle out. They are in constant tension and conversation with each other.

George: That means you can never let the matter finally or definitively be resolved.

West: Conversation goes on and on.

George: Another thing that makes it scary, especially for young people, is not knowing whether you will continue to believe what you now believe (and believe in), which is so fundamental to our sense of who we are as human beings. In addition, it's very scary to recognize that our membership in certain communities depends on maintaining belief. Communities are in part constituted by shared beliefs. So, students count themselves as members of this or that community because of the opinions they hold. I'm not just talking about religions here. I'm talking about politics, philosophy, and ideology. You're a member of this group or not, you're an insider or an outsider, depending on your beliefs.

If you put those beliefs on the table and you're really thinking, you know you may discover that you were in error and you need to change your beliefs. And that will mean you are no longer welcome in this or that community. Or if you are, you will be there merely on sufferance. You will not be a full member of that community. You will be an outsider. And young people, like the rest of us, as part of human nature, want to belong. They want to be "insiders." They want acceptance. We desperately want acceptance. And that's one of the things one is putting at risk when one really starts thinking.

Chapter Four

Truth
and
Faith

Earlier you spoke about Cardinal John Henry Newman and the idea of a university. But Newman wrote at a time when the West was Christian. In a university at that time, you could assume there was an underlying belief that we are all formed in God's image. This is a conviction that the two of you share as men of faith. But it is not widely shared today.

Cornel West: That's true.

What then is the source or ground of human dignity in the mind of a young person for whom ideology has replaced religion? Where does our fundamental respect for our fellow man—and by extension his opinions—come from?

West: These days, I think there are two dimensions of this thing that we have to talk about, because there's an existential dimension that's very different from the moral. And by existential what I mean is, what are the sources available to young people for them to cultivate the capacity for love? That's a deeper issue for me than various stories and narratives and images that provide ways in which people can affirm each other's dignity.

It's like the greatest painting in the modern West, which is Rembrandt's *The Return of the Prodigal Son.* The story's in place. All the conflict and tensions are there, but the narrative was in place. Rembrandt can take that for granted. Mennonites, Jews, and others there in the Netherlands all connect to this particular way of understanding human dignity at its deepest level. You go beyond Christianity, beyond Judaism, just human and raw, and he lays it out right before he dies, lays it down. Now jump to our period where, existentially, we got so much conformity, complacency, and cowardliness being rewarded that courage, they squeeze out. Now, courage is the enabling virtue of all the other virtues—all of them. So, even we Christians, okay, we got faith, we got hope, and the greatest of these, love. But where's courage?

None of them work without courage. You can't love without courage. God can't use cowards. You can't sustain your faith without courage. You can't go beyond the evidence with hope without courage. Kierkegaard, my dear Danish brother, wrote an essay asking, why isn't honesty a virtue among Christians? He connects it with courage, and it's a powerful reflection. Rabbi Abraham Joshua Heschel, who lived his courage when he marched with Martin Luther King at Selma, spent so much time on courage in the latter part of his last text, *A Passion for Truth*, which he wrote before he died. He says that Kierkegaard speaks to his Jewish heart because he's trying to bear witness to the courage, the mustering, the capacity to love wisdom, love beauty, love your neighbor, love the holy. What happens when you're in a culture that no longer provides that existential source and resource? We're back with Eliot again; that's probably what "Prufrock" is all about. What kind of love you got in "Prufrock"? It's barren, it's empty, it's shallow, it's hollow. What happens in such a world where narcissism cannot quite fill that void?

Robert P. George: It's self-love, and that's shallow.

West: Exactly. But there's nothing wrong with self-love if it's in a mature form. But this is narcissism in the worst sense that Christopher Lasch wrote about in *The Culture of Narcissism*, where it affects and dominates all of us. If you suffer from it, remember Dostoevsky says that Hell is suffering from the incapacity to love.

It sounds like you're saying that the modern substitute for the sense of the human being as a created subject is empathy and compassion, a sense of fellow feeling—

West: Yes, but as it runs out of gas, it gets weaker and more feeble.

George: It won't work.

West: And so what happens, exactly, is that you get the professionalism, which is all about upward mobility, it's about status and images and spectacle, and there's no existential or moral grounding that can sustain that.

George: The ur-moral principle, the foundation of all sound ethics is, in my opinion, the profound, inherent and equal dignity of each and every member of the human family. Now, why would someone believe in such a principle?

Well, if the great Hebrew insight is true that each and every member of the human family, though made from mere material stuff, the mere dust of the earth, is nevertheless fashioned in the very image and likeness of the divine creator and ruler of all that is, if that insight is true, then you've got very good grounds for believing the ur-moral principle, the profound, inherent, and equal dignity of each and every member of the human family.

The trouble is, what if you don't have that or some variant of that? Islam, strictly speaking, doesn't have the biblical story, doesn't have the idea of man being made in the image and likeness of God. But it does have man being made by God and imbued with a profound dignity as a result of his maker. So, it's close. We can see how it works in the great monotheistic traditions.

Was that the Catholic objection to slavery? That you can't buy or sell a human being because we belong to God?

George: We have to be careful and precise here. It's not because God owns you, it's because you're the kind of entity—a person, not a thing—that cannot be owned, and therefore you're not the kind of entity that can be bought and sold.

So, I'm a subject, not an object?

George: Precisely. And therefore an end, not a means. This is the key difference between *things* strictly speaking and *persons*. Human beings are persons. Islam, Christianity, and Judaism all recognize this. As creatures whose nature is rational—creatures organized for reflection, deliberation, judgment, and rationally-guided choice—human beings are godlike. They bear a quality, albeit in an imperfect and limited form, that believers attribute to God, namely, rational agency.

*In what sense are we godlike, if it's true that man
is made in the image and likeness of God?*

George: It can't be that God has five fingers on each of two
hands and hair on his head and a nose because God is spirit and
not material. So, if it's not that, if it's not our physicality that
is the godlike thing, what is the godlike thing? I think Thomas
Aquinas gets it just right. He says that what is godlike is our
capacity for reason and freedom. That's what separates us from
the brute animals, from any entity that would count as a thing
rather than a person. It's having a rational nature.

Now, we don't actually develop the immediately exercisable
capacities for rationality and freedom until fairly well along in
our lives. You don't have it as a small child or as an infant or
as an unborn child. But from the very beginning, you have a
rational nature. You are organized in such a way as to in the
fullness of time, exercise those capacities, unless a congenital
problem will mean that you will never actually develop those
capacities to the point where they're immediately exercisable.
But at least according to Jewish and Christian teaching, and I
believe the same is true in Islam, that does not mean that even
in the case of, say, a severely congenitally cognitively disabled
person, you don't have a person.

You still have a person because that individual, that creature's,
nature is a rational nature. How do we know that? Well, you
just do a simple thought experiment. If you found a way to
correct the, let's say, congenital defect that blocked the ability to
develop a fully functioning complete cognitive capacity, would
you be changing the entity from one kind of thing into another
(the way you'd be changing a horse from one sort of thing into

another if you were somehow able to cause it to talk). The thought experiment shows that if you corrected the defect, you wouldn't be changing the entity from one sort of thing into another. You wouldn't be changing his nature. You would be enabling him to fulfill his nature. You would be perfecting him as precisely the kind of thing he is.

I think that's the great Hebrew insight at the beginning of the Bible. And I think it's common to the great historical monotheistic faiths. There's not, as far as I can tell, an equivalent in the eastern faiths, in Buddhism and Hinduism, for example. But in those faiths, you do have a profound sense of the spiritual, a sense that the human being is more than merely material. The human being is understood as capable of a kind of self-transcendence through rational-spiritual practices. And in that self-transcendence, there is the foundation of dignity.

Now, when you go away from that altogether, when you abandon belief in such a thing as the spirit, the geist, then I don't know where you go. You're left with mere sentiment, with emotions. I'm as much for empathy as the next guy and I think it's very important for us to have empathy, but I don't see that as a foundational ethical principle. If we should have empathy, it must be because of some deeper principle rooted in some understanding of the human being as a bearer of dignity—

West: Having value.

George: Intrinsic value, not merely instrumental utility. That's the problem with slavery. It instrumentalizes that which is not instrumental—namely the human person. So, in respect of our animal nature, we are very similar to other animals who among the ends to which they're directed are reproduction. But because we are not merely animals, we are rational creatures, we are agents. There is a spiritual dimension of our lives. We are self-transcending. Those are the respects in which we are God-like. And even a higher animal—a dolphin, for example, or a pig, or an ape—though in a certain meaningful sense intelligent, does not manifest agency, is not a spiritual creature as far as we can see.

West: What sources are available for us to have the conception of the person as worthy of a certain kind of respect? See, in the academy today we live in the age of Lucretius, the ancient Greek who is the father of philosophical materialism. All the new breakthroughs are the new materialisms. All the new breakthroughs are new utilitarian calculations and manipulations of fueling people as atoms bouncing against each other and neutrons and protons bouncing against one another.

And you say, well, that's fascinating, and it actually holds if you're interested in prediction. The physics department will tell you exactly what a table is. It's not this aesthetic object that's fashioned in this way, it's really these electrons and neutrons. Oh, very interesting. I appreciate that. But, thank God, we can still put this water in this cup and drink it. Well, in literary criticism, humanistic studies, it's the triumph of Lucretius. It's the darkening of the humanities.

And the question is, what stories are available that can still provide justifications for us treating each other with dignity, sanctity, respect? We're not just atoms bouncing off against each other, as Lucretius thought; something else has got to be available and it's getting weaker and weaker and weaker in terms of which stories can be invoked. Now, there are Kantian stories that can be told in terms of just rational autonomy, and that's a secularized version of a certain kind of Lutheranism, saying that yes, indeed, it's no longer going to talk about God. They're just practical postulates that we can assume.

But basically, we are autonomous human beings, different from the animalistic impulses that we have, and that therefore that can serve as the basis. John Rawls's grand project—*A Theory of Justice*—is the last of the Kantian efforts in that regard, right?

George: I think that's right, and I think—

West: It's a noble thought.

George: Well, I've actually described it myself as a noble and, in a sense, even a heroic project, but one that is bound to fail and that *has* failed. Ask yourself the question, why do we across the political spectrum today believe that Alexander the Great is really not that great? Why would we not if we were starting from scratch, think of Alexander and say, "Gosh, what a great man." Why do we not admire the brutal exercise of power? Why do we not count conquest and domination as greatness? Across the spectrum, from a conservative student to the most woke student, they would say, no, no, no, that's not greatness. Why not? It certainly seemed like greatness to lots of people in the past and to lots of people in cultures unlike ours. It doesn't seem great to us because of the legacies of Christianity and Judaism.

I want to talk about the different claims of the different religions, the competing claims of the different religions, I should say. How do we think our way through those? And of course, here we have no choice but to think as individuals. We can join with each other in communities of learning and communities of inquiry. But at the end of the day, these existential questions are questions that we have to address for ourselves.

And at the risk of yet again coming across to my Brother Cornel as a hardcore rationalist, I want to plant my flag on saying that while I do appreciate what can be gleaned in the spiritual quest from music and art, there's a reason that the beautiful cathedrals are beautiful, there's a reason that beautiful hymnody is beautiful, I do think that ultimately, at the end of the day, these are questions that we have to address rationally. That, in trying to figure out an answer to the question "Where should I be religiously?", we need to use our intellects to try to figure out where we think the truth is, or where we think the truth most robustly is.

Now, having said that, I don't suppose that we begin by trying to take "the view from nowhere." I think Alasdair MacIntyre has taught us something profoundly true when he teaches us that we always begin from a tradition that provides the intellectual resources on which we rely in the project of thinking. That tradition might be a religious one, it might be a secular one. It could even be an anti-religious one. He himself has the experience of Marxism, being a Marxist operating from that tradition before he personally abandoned it, eventually embracing Catholic Christianity. But even in thinking his way out of Marxism and into Christianity, he was drawing on certain resources of the Marxist tradition to subject that tradition to scrutiny and decide whether to stick with it or leave it behind.

And interestingly—and I think MacIntyre is right about this too—although you might think that drawing on the resources of a tradition will mean that you will always be reinforced in the teachings of the tradition, it actually doesn't work out that way in human experience. In drawing on the resources of traditions we may find ourselves confronted with the reality that the tradition in which we were brought up or the tradition to which we have given our allegiance, generates serious questions or problems that it lacks the resources to address. MacIntyre says that at that point, from our vantage point as inquirers, the tradition goes into what he calls an epistemological crisis.

He develops these ideas in his book, *Whose Justice? Which Rationality?* He observes that in an epistemological crisis, one is forced to look around, to inquire, to criticize the tradition, to note the problems that the tradition has identified and can't answer or address. And the net result might be, as it has been in his own case more than once, to catapult him out of that tradition into a different tradition which can handle the question without raising other questions that that tradition itself can't handle. So, the MacIntyre who was once a logical positivist and once a Marxist ends up being a Thomist and a Catholic.

My point is that each of us, in asking "Where should I be religiously?" should be using the old noggin, using the intellect, assessing the claims from a rational point of view, even claims of revelation. After all, there are reasons we can have for believing or disbelieving that a certain thing was revealed. Those are matters of historical inquiry in many cases. Like, did Jesus rise from the dead? That's a historical question. There are data that are available to enable you or me or anyone else to assess that claim.

But while I think that we should be using our intellects to try to figure out where truth lies in the religious domain, just as we do in the scientific or other domains, we don't start from nowhere.

We begin from within a tradition. It might be the one we were born in. It might be one that we have previously converted into. But we're drawing on the resources of some tradition to think. You cannot think in complete abstraction from any tradition.

West: Okay, but I'm going to invoke a Catholic against you here.

George: Go for it, my brother.

West: I'm thinking of the great Giambattista Vico. Vico says that wisdom began with the muse, and wisdom begins in the history of songs. He's going back to Homer. Homer is a number of different figures and voices over time who are constellating and crystallizing this unbelievable *phronesis*. By the time you get to Plato in Book 10 of the *Republic*, the traditional quarrel between poetry and philosophy is really Plato versus Homer. Plato is trying to displace Homer as the teacher of wisdom and virtue and replace him with Socrates. And how do I displace Homer as the source of this *paideia*, this education that people need to undergo to get that wisdom? It begins with Orpheus, in music, the lyre, the stories. So that even in those churches that you talk about, they're empty if there's no music and no stories there.

George: I agree with that. I'm not downplaying it.

West: So, what I'm saying is, rationality is intertwined with all that other stuff that's hard to subsume under the rational. You see what I mean? This is not anti-rational, it's just situating rationality. And Vico, as a Catholic, already knows the centrality of the arts, of the storytellers, of the poets, of the bards, and so forth. And he sees this on the way to what Robby's talking about: It's on the way to rational discourse. It's on the way to the kind of clarifying that you're talking about, evidence adducing activity.

George: I can see the importance of all that and I don't want to downplay it at all. But at the end of the day, one has to make a judgment. There is no way around that. And I think this is what held up Chekhov at the end. He saw the beauty, he understood—

West: Well, he saw the existential truth without accepting the Christian conclusion.

George: That's right. But he couldn't in the end bring himself to make the jump.

West: He wasn't a Christian, we understand. I can understand it, brother. Definitely. He was a Darwinian medical doctor.

George: Oh no, I'm not even criticizing him at the moment. I'm just noting the necessity, the unavoidability, of making a judgment.

West: Right. No, no, but I mean—let's assume that Chekhov should have believed, just for the sake of argument, what we believe he should have. It would've been better had he made the judgment and embraced belief.

George: Well, of course, I disagree with his agnosticism—with the judgment he happens to have made.

West: Disbelief, right?

George: Now what didn't happen that should have happened— it wasn't that he failed to appreciate the beauty of poetry or music. He didn't make the intellectual judgment that needed to be made (assuming for the moment and for the sake of argument that the judgment you and I make and he declined to make is the correct judgment from the rational point of view).

West: A dose of rationality is not going to do it, though. That's not going to be the thing to push him over the line to join us in the Christian club.

George: It's his own criterion, right? He wants to know why I should believe it, because it's too beautiful to be true.

West: Yeah, because he was just not convinced of the narrative.

George: Wait, convinced, see there's the word!

West: Well, that's true. *Peitho*, which goes all the way back to the Greeks. *Peitho* is persuasion. That's at the center of it right?

George: That's judgment. It's an act of the intellect.

West: That's the thing that allows us within that space of reasons, that zone of rational persuasion. But when people get in there, the evidence is always under-determined.

George: I see where you're going, but we're going to reach disagreement on this one!

West: It's always under-determined. The evidence for the Resurrection is under-determined. Brother Robert, you got to make a leap of faith.

George: No!

West: You think it's just rational evidence to lead you to believe in the Resurrection?

George: Exactly.

West: No! No!

George: There's that Protestant sensibility coming out.

West: No!

George: But you assess the credibility of the witnesses.

West: But in the eyes of God....

George: No, we don't have God's eyes, we have our own eyes.

West: And so, we don't need to have evidence in our eyes, because what God is doing is so far beyond anything we can conceive. If we have rational evidence for the Resurrection, what makes it the miracle that it is?

George: Nobody would believe in the Resurrection today, including you and me, if we did not have the testimony of the apostles, and my point is that either we believe the credibility of their testimony or we don't.

West: Well, I hear what you're saying, but let me just quote a letter from the exemplary irrationalist Dostoevsky himself. You remember that letter he writes where he says that if all reality and evidence were on one side and Jesus Christ was on the other, I'm going for Jesus? Now, I'm not that kind of irrationalist, but I appreciate Dostoevsky for it. Because it's not going to be the evidence of whatever's there that's going to push you. The only thing that's going to push you is—actually it's best represented in the next to last paragraph of David Hume's great classic, the *Dialogues Concerning Natural Religion*.

Now, here you get this lapsed Presbyterian to the core who's not valorizing reason. He's Scottish Enlightenment, but he's *phronesis*; he's practical reason all the way. And what does he say? He says, the only way a Christian can believe in the Christian faith is if they undergo a miracle in the transformation of their lives in relation to something bigger than them. That's not just the testimony of the disciples. It's something that's happened in your own life. You know you have been converted because you were such a gangster and a thug, and this blood at the cross has transformed you into a redeemed sinner with gangster proclivities.

George: But you've got to believe that the story is true.

West: Yes, that's true.

George: You've got to be persuaded.

West: But not evidentially.

George: What other way is there?

West: Leaps of faith.

George: Even in the first century, the reason that people believed was they believed the testimony of the apostles and the women and men who had actually seen Jesus crucified and experienced his coming to them having risen from the dead.

How did the Catholic Church manage heresy? In some cases, the church created monastic orders to accommodate charismatic figures like Francis and Dominic. Others they burned as heretics. But they had to make an executive decision about how they were going to handle the challenge to the orthodox truth from someone's personal revelation.

West: You remember G.K. Chesterton's great book *Orthodoxy*. Orthodoxy is even more Socratic. It's not static and stationary, but it is rooted in the best of what one understands the past to be, to inform the continuity of the traditions.

George: The other point Chesterton makes is that heresies are not flat-out falsehoods. Heresies are schools of thought that place so much emphasis on one side of a complex truth that they suppress the other side or sides. So, for example, the orthodox position is that Jesus is both God and man. You can have a heresy on either side—seeing Jesus only as God, which some early Christian heretics did, or seeing Jesus only as a man, as others did. And you can go through all the heresies and you find the same. You're going all the way back to Irenaeus' critique of the Gnostic heretics.

Say more about it, because there's been a lot of talk lately about Gnosticism having a recrudescence in the form of wokeism.

George: What most Christians know and are taught about Gnostics is that they believed that they held secret knowledge, and that's certainly true, and it's a very important dimension of their thought. And, of course, that's something antithetical to the teachings of orthodox Christianity, whether it's east or west, Protestant or Catholic. In Christianity, there's no secret knowledge or elite that has the secret knowledge from which everybody else is excluded. It's a very important thing about Christianity. That's why the Gnostics had to be declared heretics.

There's an aspect of Gnosticism that I think is experiencing a recrudescence today that people know less about, and that is the Gnostic division of the human being into a material body which is sub-personal reality and a psyche or spirit or soul or center of consciousness and feeling that is the "true" person. So, the Gnostics embraced the basic idea that human beings are "ghosts in machines," and the real person is the ghost, not the machine. The machine is a sub-personal instrument of the real person considered as the spiritual substance, the psyche or the soul at the center of consciousness.

The real person sort of inhabits the body the way a driver might inhabit a car and turn the steering wheel and hit the gas and make the car go left or right or straight or what have you. The orthodox Christian response was to embrace a version of the Aristotelian view of these matters, which is known as hylomorphism. In the hylomorphic view, which I've defended in my own writings, the person cannot be reduced either to the spiritual aspects of the self or the material aspects of the self. Rather, the person is a body-soul or body-mind composite. The body is every bit as much a part of the personal reality of the human being as the mind or psyche or spirit or soul. So, from the orthodox Christian point of view, if you have a human body, if you *are* a human body, then you are a person.

There's not a period when you have a human body, but are not yet a person.

Peter Singer, who you mentioned earlier, would say that a newborn infant is not yet a person. Singer would certainly allow that he or she is a human being. That's just a biological fact, and he's critical of people who try to deny it. It's scientifically undeniable. But he insists that being a human being is not enough for a creature to be a bearer of worth, and thus count for purposes of his utilitarian calculations. Something more is needed, namely, a certain level of mental functioning, one that is not attained by a child until some months after birth (and which may be lost even before death). That's why he believes that infanticide (as well as, of course, abortion) is morally permissible or at least involves no wrongdoing or injustice to the child who is killed at his or her parents' request. He or she is not (yet), in Singer's view, a "person." He or she is a human non-person. If you perceive certain resonances here with the person-body dualism characteristic of Gnosticism, you wouldn't be wrong.

Of course, I see things entirely differently. Since a newborn human being (and, indeed, an unborn human being, as Singer agrees) is a human being, that individual is (and on this point Singer disagrees) a bearer of inherent and equal dignity—a person—even though he or she cannot yet speak in sentences, conduct inquiries, have a level of self-awareness of the sort he or she will later attain if allowed to live. This is what it means to say that his or her nature, as a human being, is a rational nature. There are no human beings who are "not yet" persons. By the same token, there cannot be no post-personal human beings, that is, human beings who were once persons but are now no longer persons because of dementia or a severe cognitive disability or because they are in a coma or anything like that.

Singer again would say, "Sure. Uncle Henry, who's suffering from Alzheimer's disease, is a human being. That's a matter of biological fact. But he's no longer a person. He once was, but he is no longer." What Singer is embracing here is very much in line with the person-body dualism, the self-body dualism, that was at the heart of Gnostic philosophical anthropology. Now the various Gnostic sects disagreed among themselves as to the moral implications of this anthropology.

West: Absolutely.

George: Some saw the body as bad.

West: Absolutely.

George: And the goal was to lead a profoundly ascetic life, one that rejected bodily pleasures. For others, it was the opposite. Since the body doesn't really matter, debauchery was perfectly fine. What needed to be kept pure was the soul. The debauchery so often glamorized and celebrated in our time seems to be founded upon a similar view of the human body and its relation to the rational-spiritual dimensions of the human person. Since the body doesn't really matter all that much, you can't commit sexual sins unless there is coercion or deception involved. As long as your spirit is pure, your intentions are good, your mind is pure, it's "no harm, no foul." The sole criterion of right and wrong in sexual matters is consent.

West: I do think it's important to keep track of both the truth of Gnosticism and what some of the motivation of Gnostics is. It's because they have such a catastrophic conception of creation, of history, of materiality, of corporality. All those are poor vessels for transcendence. If you look at human history, you might get some moments of joy and happiness, but you also get wars, hatred, greed, and so forth. You look at the body: It's in a process of constant decay, and it's like what James Joyce said about history, the nightmare from which he's trying to awake. So, where else do you go?

So again, it's one-sided, but at a moment in which the sense of catastrophe is so overwhelming that people are looking for an escape from history, escape from body, escape from materiality, Gnosticism does make sense, because history is catastrophic. I mean, the vessels that are shattered in Kabbalistic cosmology, which is the Jewish form of Gnosticism—they're shattered at the very beginning and you're trying to regather all those pieces. It's like trying to put Humpty Dumpty together. No. Humpty Dumpty fell. You can't put him together again. And the literary critic Harold Bloom, who was also a great Emersonian Gnostic, would be the first to say, well, thank God for Emerson, because at least you've got a conception of self-creation that's tied to genius, that's tied to traditions of geniuses that can provide ways in which we could cope with this catastrophe. There's something to be said for that, I must say.

George: I can understand why Gnosticism's dualistic understanding of the human being would have appeal in an age of feeling, an age of radical subjectivity. The real "me" is regarded as the conscious and desiring part of the self. That's what really matters. The rest of this stuff is just "material" and therefore purely instrumental, so I can use it as a tool. I can manipulate it. You find this probably in its most advanced form in the aspirations and utopian ambitions of the transhumanists and get rid of the body altogether. We can live by downloading our consciousness (our true selves) into computers.

West: Right.

George: You can also see it in the idea that I might be a biologically male human being, but I might be a psychically female human being. Or in the idea that what unites persons is not their bodily joining, say in a marital union, but simply the union at the level of feeling or emotion, the psychic level. So, I think some of the challenges that you get to traditional Judeo-Christian ethical teachings come from this neo-Gnostic dualism.

West: But you can imagine though, if you have a patriarchal God or a white supremacist God or anti-Jewish God and so forth, then people will experience that God in a catastrophic way.

George: Absolutely.

West: And they have to come up with some creative response to it, you see. All I'm saying is that, again, it's a matter of trying to stay in contact with the complexity of each position and to have truths that can be semblances of truths and the overarching narrow truths that can generate responses because they're not attending to certain dimensions of who we are, what our history is.

George: Let me conclude with a story. I remember once in a class Cornel and I were teaching, we were reading St. Augustine's *Confessions*. We were deep in the conversation wrestling with some of the questions with which Augustine wrestles—some very dark aspects of the human condition and the real challenges of what it means to be a human being. Martin Luther and the reformers claim Augustine because of his deep sense of just how fallen human beings are, just how bad we are, just how deeply original sin has deformed us. Of course, that's why we require redemption.

I noticed at one point that one of our students had tears coming down her face, and I was a little worried about that. I didn't say anything because I didn't want to embarrass her. But when we had a coffee break, I immediately went over to her and took her aside, and asked her, "Are you all right? I noticed that you were weeping." And she said, "Well, I had never read Augustine before and never really discussed in a deep way the issues that we're discussing today. And it just relates to my own struggles in life so directly and immediately."

And that's why she was weeping. The book was having such an impact on her. This is not a kid who was just looking for an interesting course and hoping to get an A because she was going to go to law school or whatever. She was genuinely affected, heart and mind and soul, by this discussion, by the ideas of this guy who died a millennium and a half ago. Well, the next thing I knew, she was in touch with me to say that she had been reflecting on her own faith and had decided she wanted to become a Catholic and asked for some guidance about who she might talk with. I put her in touch with the campus chaplain and she decided to become a Catholic. She asked me if I would be her godfather, which I was very honored by and agreed to do.

She then got in touch with Brother Cornel to ask if he would come to the Easter Vigil service during which she would be among those received into the Catholic Church, the catechumens or the converts. Cornel said of course he'd be delighted. So, we attended the Easter Vigil in Trenton Cathedral. We sat up in the front row with her and the other people who were being received into the Catholic Church. Getting Cornel in and out was a bit of a challenge because this was Trenton, New Jersey, and the congregation knew exactly who Cornel was, and they were delighted and stunned that he was there. People were just descending on him from all over.

West: Who is this Black Baptist going into this Catholic cathedral?

George: Catholic Masses are usually not very long, less than an hour. But at the Easter Vigil, we do it right. So, it was a three-hour ceremony. I remember Cornel turned to me at one point, struck by all the majesty and grandeur and everything, and he said, "Brother Robby, we Baptists, we're just a little rowboat. This is like being on a great ocean liner."

West: A huge ocean liner.

George: In any case, the point came in the ceremony when the catechumens, the converts, were called up to individually come to the altar where the bishop was seated on his throne-like chair with his crozier. And the bishop would do the formal receiving of the catechumen into the Catholic Church. And the tradition is that the godparent comes and puts a hand on his or her shoulder. When the young lady and I were called up, Brother Cornel whispers to me, "Can I come too?" And I said, "Sure, of course." The two of us accompanied her as she knelt before the bishop and I put my hand on her right shoulder, and Cornel put his hand on her left shoulder, and the bishop looked at Cornel and gave him a great big smile, and he did the blessing and received her into the church.

West: It really was beautiful.

George: I tell this story because it shows that there are students who are really interested in the substance of the questions, the deep and important questions. They're not all simply interested in getting ahead and getting that Ivy League degree, and going to Harvard Business School and on to Goldman Sachs, or Yale Law School, and on to Cravath, Swaine & Moore. Not that we discourage students from aspiring to careers in business or law or anything like that. That's fine. But we also want them to actually get an education and benefit from it. That means wrestling with the great existential questions.

Chapter Five

Confronting Truth in History

Let's take a contemporary question that bears on many people's political beliefs. Does history have an arc? Does that arc bend toward justice? One could argue that in the context of Western civilization, at least, there has been moral progress toward realizing liberal ideals. What is your view as men of Christian faith about history and morality? Is history taking us anywhere?

Robert P. George: I don't think that history has an arc. I don't think history has a direction. Yes, we sometimes make moral progress, but sometimes we progress in one area and decline in another. I think that the Hegelian idea picked up by Marx that there's a direction of history or that you could be, as President Barack Obama would warn his political opponents, on the wrong rather than right side of history, is just a mistake. I think history is a sequence of contingent events, always depending in very significant ways on the choices of human beings. What's more, history has no more power to judge the morality of our actions than has a stone outcropping or a painted totem pole.

In some ways, the idea of an arc of history or that history has a right and a wrong side is modern secularism's effort to find a replacement for the idea of divine judgment. Really, at the end of the day, it's a silly attempt to replace the idea of a God who renders judgment with history in the role of God. It threatens the "heretic" with the judgment of history.

Cornel West: Niall Ferguson says that there have roughly been about seventy empires in the history of the species since emerging from the caves and each imperial civilization has its own internal dynamics. They may have had their own mini arcs, but the mini arcs are not following Martin Luther King's ideal of bending toward justice. They can move toward justice in one sphere, and move toward injustice in another. They could move toward beauty or move toward terror. What's distinctive about the West is that the West was able to reshape so much of the world in its image and various interests. Empires have been doing that from the very beginning. I mean, the Persian Empire was no joke, the Mongolian Empire was no joke. The Roman Empire—oh my God—Cato and Cicero against Julius Caesar? There's Republic against Empire. All these have internal dynamics. This is true in Africa, Asia, and among Indigenous peoples and so forth.

I think you're right to say that the West picked up on moral arc talk in a powerful way because it had a range and a scope given the instrumentalities of its nation-states, its militaries, its republic of letters, its languages, the very language we speak. So, in that sense, I'm with Brother Robby. I do think we want to have a certain skepticism about any moral arc talk. I think human beings are so wretched—and we're wonderful in potential—we're so wretched that the arc could be the planet not existing anymore, it could be Nagasakis and Hiroshimas everywhere. We don't know. History is unpredictable, it's incomplete. It depends on what we do in that way.

George: You're right, and very much in the tradition of our founders, who knew they were proposing an experiment in republican government and ordered liberty, and knew that by definition experiments can fail. There's no guarantee that ours will succeed. It is quite remarkable that it has succeeded for as long as it has, especially given the stresses and strains. It almost failed in the period from 1861 to 1865. There was even earlier a real question of whether it would survive the presidential and congressional election campaigns of 1800. A bitter, bitter election. In our own time, I think we're facing the question again. Could it fail? Yes, it could fail. You see this in the extreme polarization of our politics and culture. I think it's probably the worst since the Civil War, not yet to the point where we'll have a civil war. And I pray that that would never again happen. But I think it's as bad as it has been since the 1860s.

I don't think the experiment can succeed if we lose our sense of the metaphysical and moral foundations of the American experiment, the proposition that all men are created equal and endowed by their Creator with certain unalienable rights. To write a statement like that now would be very controversial. It would divide us, which shows you that we are in a rather desperate situation, because for most of our history, at least since the Civil War, people were united in believing Thomas Jefferson's proposition. Whether they happened to like or dislike Jefferson himself, they agreed with his proposition.

The Civil War defeated the famous claim of Alexander Stephens, the secessionist politician and vice president of the Confederacy, who said that not only is the Jeffersonian proposition not self-evidently true, it's self-evidently false. In defending slavery, Stephens claimed that it just wasn't true that all men are created equal—that the American republic is built on a false claim.

When I was younger, in the wake of World War II—my father served in Normandy and Brittany—whatever the differences between Republicans and Democrats, liberals and conservatives and so forth, across the different faiths, Americans were united in believing in Jefferson's proposition.

Could anybody write such a statement today?

George: Today I think it would be controversial, very controversial. Now, having said all that, one of the things this points to—and this is an insight that goes back to Alexis de Tocqueville—is the importance of the institutions of civil society, especially families and religious communities, churches, and other religious institutions in sustaining the cultural, moral, and religious bases of American life. Today we would say democracy; our framers would have favored the term republicanism. Our founders understood that there were social conditions that had to be in place for the political system they put in place, this Republican civic order, to succeed. Those conditions are nurtured and sustained by institutions and individuals outside of the political system, moms and dads, grandmas and grandpas, priests and ministers and rabbis, coaches and teachers, and the like.

*Didn't the founders take for granted that people
would continue to be religious, to believe in God,
and that this would ensure a certain level of
morality and decency in the public at large?*

George: The reason the Declaration resonated with people is that they agreed that our fundamental rights, and we should add duties, are not the gifts of kings, or parliaments, or presidents, or congresses. They are not given to us by any merely human power. And because they are not the gift of any merely human power, they cannot legitimately be taken away by any merely human power. The king or the president, the Parliament or the Congress, stand under the judgment of the moral law because the moral law was not created by the king or the Parliament, or the president or the Congress.

When Martin Luther King in 1963, writing from the Birmingham Jail, asked himself the question, "How do we know the difference between just and unjust laws?" he says, "I would be the first to say we have a moral as well as a legal obligation to obey just laws. But I think we have a moral obligation to disobey unjust laws." He asks, "How do you tell the difference between the two?" And he says, "Well, just laws are laws that are in line with natural law and the law of God. Unjust laws are laws that are out of line with the natural law and the law of God." The natural law and the law of God are the laws that uphold the flourishing of the human personality. In the "Letter from Birmingham Jail," he used the term "Personality," in other places, he used the term " spirit." In other words, just laws uplift the human spirit, the human personality. Unjust laws degrade them. They degrade the human spirit of the victim, and also—and this is important—of the victimizer. They dehumanize the ostensible beneficiaries of injustice (e.g., the slaveholders) as well as its victims.

Now, on that, you can build a republican civic order. We can have government not only of the people, which all government is, and not only for the people, which all good government is, even if it's the rule of a benign despot, but government by the people—that is, republican government. Of course, in a republican civic order, the people are themselves, in a certain sense, sovereign. But it will only work if the people understand that, though sovereign in one sense, they are subject to a higher law, what King had in mind when he referred to "the natural law and the law of God." Even the sovereign people are answerable. Without that accountability, that sense of accountability, that perception of being subject to something higher, republicanism will do what it always did prior to the American experiment.

West: Fail or degenerate.

George: And when it fails, it will degenerate into the worst forms of tyranny.

West: The worst forms of tyranny. But I would add one other crucial dimension here, and I would say that the genius of American culture, life, society, is its jazz-like practices. And by jazz-like, what I mean is experimental, improvisational, flexible, fluid, protean. You can have the most beautiful things written on paper and still have forms of domination, slavery, subjugation in place.

So, the question becomes, then, are you open to unleash Socratic energy to critically reflect upon yourself as a social experiment, to be jazz-like in your practices? There's a wonderful essay by the great Tennessee Williams called "The Catastrophe of Success," in which he was saying in part that every success has built into it forms of failure. Yes, Indigenous peoples, Black people, women, poor white workers, and so forth. And they would say, "Well, it doesn't look too successful from here." Now, people would have their own comparative analysis. Maybe the peasants from Italy would say, "It's better than Sicily, but I'm still catching hell." Or the Africans would say, "I think I may rather be in Africa, rather than dying at twenty-seven years old for 244 years under this barbaric slavery."

But you have to be able to see this interplay, this intricate interplay between success and failure. And if you're not improvisational and jazz-like, able to use the strengths of your success to speak to the dimness of the failures, you're going to end up collapsing anyway. That's part of what 1861 was about, right? You're going to end up fighting over an institution not invoked in your constitution because the constitution has a compromise of a certain silence about the 22 percent of the inhabitants who were enslaved, and their labor would be one of the preconditions for democracy, just like the land of Indigenous peoples.

So, the question becomes, how do we attempt to be truthful? Herman Melville's right when he says that truth is a jagged edge, a Janus-faced phenomenon. So, if you just want to talk about the truth, it's going to cut us as well as cut others, and it's always bigger than all of us. And what jazz-like practices do is to say, given these powerful metaphysical foundations, given these powerful stories about equality, how does it translate on the ground? I mean, if the Constitution is pro-slavery in practice between 1789 and 1863, you say, "We got to come to terms with that." You got slaveholders who are president, slaveholders on the supreme court, slaveholders in the courts, and so on and so forth. So, you have to be able to say, "I think we must have our groundings and bases in place, but we must also be experimental and flexible enough in our practices to acknowledge how our successes can hide and conceal our failures."

George: I agree with all that. And here I would commend the vision of the founders. Again, whatever their personal faults and limitations, and even in terms of their political vision, they were still remarkable. The ideas that they came up with—they wouldn't have put it in Cornel's terms of being jazz-like and improvisational—but that's the constitutional system. It's making sure that nobody or no one institution has unchecked and unlimited power. It's separating powers even within the national government, and then restricting the national government to its delegated and enumerated powers. Leaving all other powers to the states and to the people respectively in our system of federalism.

So, you've got room for experimentation. You don't have to do things in Montana the same way you do them in Missouri, Mississippi, or Massachusetts. Also, you have—I'll borrow a term from Karl Popper—an open society—at least when we are true to our constitutional commitments. The Constitution not only leaves room for the institutions of civil society, it protects them so that they can function autonomously and with their own integrity and not under the thumb of the government. And in those families and churches and civic associations of every description, there's an enormous amount of room for innovation, for organizing, for attacking what we perceive to be injustices and wrongs.

West: Abolitionist movements.

George: Exactly. Women suffrage movements, temperance, the campaigns against child labor and for civil rights.

West: Absolutely.

George: And also, even where there's not an injustice to be challenged, we reasonably and rightly rely on the institutions of civil society to accomplish certain ends that we think it's best not to pursue through a regimented government system. We leave room for alternative approaches, new ideas, experimentation, creative ways of approaching problems. We don't need a national government-run little league. We can let little league operate with local autonomy and private initiative, organization, and management. The same is true when it comes to some areas of health, education, and welfare.

I think it's good that we have a governmental social safety net, but I also think it's important for civil society to have a lot of room and incentives to provide health, education, and welfare, and to care for the needy. We know as a matter of practice that faith-based institutions consistently do better than the government in providing care for the least, the last, and the lost. Now, that's not to say we should eliminate the governmental safety net. As I say, I support it. But I don't want that safety net to displace the institutions of civil society or eliminate their role in the provision of care for the needy.

There's an implicit argument here against the utopian impulse to create a perfect society. That is, we have to allow for human imperfection, for venal impulses. We have a system that allows people the maximum amount of liberty and, really, the liberty to be bad people in a way, up to a point where it becomes a problem for others.

George: I think we're rightly concerned politically with the character of our people. John Adams said that ours is a constitution that will work only for a moral and religious people and will not serve for any other. There are certain conditions for the constitutional system working and virtue in the people is one of them. In fact, in the Federalist papers, we're taught that the structural constraints on governmental power, the separation of powers for example, are auxiliary. They're not the primary protections of liberty and the integrity of the republican civic order for the system. What are the primary ones? The virtues of the people. Now, can the government create virtue in people? No. All it can do is support, play a subsidiary role in supporting families and churches and other institutions of civil society that will play the main role in transmitting to each new generation the virtues necessary for the people of that generation to lead successful lives and be good republican citizens.

This introduces the concept of subsidiarity, which I think is really important to our understanding of how a good republican civic order works. That's the idea that problems should be solved as close to the people whose problems they are as possible. If an individual can handle a problem himself, let him handle it. A good parent will not step in to do the kid's math homework. The kid has to do his own homework because that's the only way he'll learn to do math. Now, if he's having trouble, dad or mom will step in and help or maybe get him a tutor or something like that. But to the extent that the individual can handle it, you let him, because it's better for him.

If a family can handle a problem and you don't need the neighborhood association or the larger community to manage it, let the family handle the problem. If the family can't handle it, but the community can—let's say we don't have enough recreational facilities or we don't have a library in our community, and it would be good to have these facilities but no one family can afford it—well, the families all get together and work to provide a good that will serve the entire community. Now, there are certain problems that can't be resolved by private initiative, and then government has to step in. Even there, according to the doctrine or principle of subsidiarity, the problem should be solved at the lowest level of government at which it can be solved, basically because it's safer for the people for power to be exercised as close to them as possible. Government needs to be accountable to them, or they will soon find themselves subjected to tyranny.

If a problem can't be handled locally, it's got to go up to the provincial or state level. If it can't be managed there, it's got to be done at the national level. Now, with all this, we have to bear in mind a couple of things that I'm sure Cornel would quickly point out if I don't. Number one is of course, sometimes you have abuses at the level at which powers are being exercised, which cannot be eradicated without a higher authority stepping in. That can be public power, but it can also be private power. You can have wealthy interests, for example, exercising power in a way that is truly exploitative and abusive.

The only way you can protect people from that exploitation and abuse by private power is by exercising governmental power against the private power. Now, the trick is *prudentia*. It's prudence. It's knowing when government should step in and when government shouldn't, and there's no formula for that. There's no algorithm. This requires the judgment of a statesman. Unfortunately, statesmanship is—

West: Rare, very, very rare.

George: If we had a libertarian friend here with us, he would make the following point. He would say, "Oh, that's all very good. But you have to remember this in exercising your prudence: Once government steps in to solve a problem or rectify a wrong, it won't then step out once the problem has been solved. It becomes an interest in itself, which will inevitably be self-aggrandizing. You'll just create a ratchet where you get more and more government and less and less liberty."

Of course, liberty is what the libertarian is rightly focused on and concerned about. In this vale of tears, there's no easy solution to these problems. Reasonable people of goodwill in the concrete circumstances can reasonably disagree about whether government should be stepping in here or whether the matter should be left to private initiative and resolution. And even if the decision is that government intervention is warranted, we face the question of or at what level of government should address the problem.

West: That's why in some ways when you look at American history it's dotted with waves of spiritual awakenings and moral reckonings, which are rooted in civil institutions putting pressure on concentrated power in high places. That could be in the public sphere of government. It could be the private sphere with greedy corporate elites or professional elites or what have you. These spiritual awakenings and moral reckonings are ideologically promiscuous.

George: That's right.

West: You see, people think that they're always progressive and good and virtuous. No. Now, fascism is a certain kind of spiritual awakening, it is just tied to something that we think is demonic and hateful. That has to do again with the geist of the folk. It is the spirit of the folk, how are they cultivating certain kinds of capacities, what forms of education, what forms of *paideia* are they trying to enact?

Paideia—education—has to do with this formation of attention. It has to do with the cultivation of critical sensibilities, has to do with the maturation of compassionate personalities. If your *paideia* is truncated, as the present one is—technocratic, careerist, opportunist, and a whole host of other things—it's going to be devastating. It's going to be lethal. That's part of the spiritual decay we're wrestling with today.

But there are other ways in which spiritual awakening can be much broader. They take all these different forms and we're back to Robby's arcs of history again. You see these arcs get confused because they're happening simultaneously in this way. That's why democracies are so fragile and tend not to last that long. It takes a tremendous amount of cultivation of people's capacities.

This is where Cicero I think is crucial. He's got this notion of a true sage, of the orator who is able to defend the best of a heritage, to speak to the best of a people. It's very rare, but it's also crucial especially in a republic or a democracy. When you think of Abraham Lincoln in his role as an orator and teacher, the American experiment without him is over. It's over.

George: It almost didn't survive his assassination.

West: Cicero writes that the orator has to have the subtleties of the logician, the concepts of the philosopher, the lawyer's memory, the diction of the poet, and the consummate abilities of an actor to instruct and move the people toward democratic ends. That's Cicero himself at his height. That's heavy stuff.

George: That's all in Lincoln's second inaugural address.

West: That is sublime.

George: Sublime. I think it's clearest—or at least most evident—in the magnanimity of the speech.

West: Absolutely.

George: The victory is in sight. He knows at that point that the Union will prevail and the experiment will continue. He says at the beginning of the speech that we all know that our progress of arms is satisfactory. Victory is in sight. Now, an ordinary politician would be beating his chest saying, "Hurrah, hurrah, hurrah for us"—really meaning hurrah for *me*; re-elect me. But at the risk of losing his audience, which was not in a magnanimous mood toward the Confederacy, he essentially announces a policy of non-judgmentalism. He says that both sides worship the same God. Both sides prayed to Him for a victory. He couldn't give both sides what they wanted and has given neither side fully what it wanted. He says that "I don't see how you could demand justice from a just God while you're winning your bread from the sweat of another man's brow." There's a shot at slavery. Then, however, he quotes the Bible, "But let us judge not lest we be judged."

Then he states that the war is a punishment on both sides—not just the south, but on both sides—for the sin of slavery. Then, he concludes by saying, "with malice towards none; with charity for all." Charity for all means charity for the *rebels*, the *defeated* rebels. Then he invokes their common journey forward: "Let us strive on to finish the work we are in, to bind up the nation's wounds, to care for him who shall have borne the battle and for his widow and his orphan, to do all which may achieve and cherish a just and lasting peace among ourselves and with all nations." *This* is statesmanship.

Bringing it back to your role as teachers preparing young people to be citizens of a democracy, do you want your students to "change the world" and make the world a better place?

George: Oh yes. We want them to be good citizens. We want them to leave the world at least a little better than they found it by virtue of their contributions. No question about that. Does that include standing for justice where there is injustice? Absolutely. But as important as that is, especially when we know that they're also very focused at this stage on their own futures, their careers, and their ambitions for wealth and status and so forth, I think it's important that we help them understand that the greatest challenge they will face through their entire lives, and the most important thing that they need to accomplish, is self-mastery.

That doesn't excuse them from the obligation to make the world a better place, to be a blessing to their community, first to their families and the families they will form. But the biggest challenge they will face, the challenge all of us face, lies in overcoming one's own wayward desires, feelings, emotions, passions. Being master of oneself, getting reason in control of passion.

Cornel mentioned David Hume. Speaking of human motivation, Hume famously (or infamously) said that, "Reason is and ought only to be the slave of the passions and may pretend to no office other than to serve and obey them." Here he is really echoing Thomas Hobbes, who said that, "The thoughts are to the desires as scouts and spies to range abroad and find the way to the thing desired." Not only are Hobbes and Hume wrong about that, not only is it possible for us to be masters of ourselves, for reason to be in control of desire, our first and most fundamental obligation and our biggest challenge is to make it so. To be people for whom reason is in control of desire.

Although I'm a great respecter of the Buddhist tradition—and I've studied Buddhism formally, especially the Theravada tradition—and while I am a great admirer of especially the Roman Stoic philosophers, I don't believe that our task is to eliminate desire or emotion, to squeeze it out of our lives. I do think that a rich and full human life will have its affective dimensions, and that those are important. But the most important thing is to make sure that our passions are properly ordered. They're not controlling us, we are controlling them. Reason is in charge of passion, we have that self-control. That's another way of saying, the most important thing they'll ever do is form a virtuous character.

West: You see, my dear brother, you're sounding very much like our beloved Greek pagans. Aristotle talks about self-mastery, and I do understand it in the Thomistic tradition, but for me it's more self-surrender than self-mastery. I don't think that human beings have the rational capacity to actually be in control, with that chariot that Plato describes in the *Republic* with the three levels of the soul, you see. The rational, the spirited, and the appetitive. I don't think human beings have what it takes for that. And without grace, without a gift from outside, self-surrender can generate a particular kind of ordering that looks like, let's say Christian self-mastery versus Platonic self-mastery, Aristotelian self-mastery, Socratic self-mastery. But the language of self-mastery, I try to hold at arm's length, because our wretchedness is not good news. You tell a wretched creature to have self-mastery but they live in chaos and have no idea how to proceed and how to do it. No, they need some help.

George: At a certain level this is a Protestant-Catholic difference as well as a difference of temperament.

West: But see, the thing about the rich Catholic tradition, Blaise Pascal is—

George: He's leaning your way. Pascal as a skeptic has a dimmer view of the power of reason than I think we can and should affirm.

West: And Augustine.

George: Oh, for sure. There's very little in the Protestant tradition that is not pre-figured in some aspects of the thought of pre-Reformation Catholic thinkers.

West: Exactly. Catholics, their tradition is so rich, and it's part of my tradition, too, as a Christian, but it's so rich that St. Francis of Assisi is as close a comrade as I can get, and so is Dorothy Day, who all her life wrestled with nihilism, wrestled with melancholy, wrestled with despair and darkness and bleakness, but she allowed the love, the community, to have the last words. But about self-surrender: Self-surrender is an acknowledgement of one's wretchedness, of one's sinfulness, of one falling so short of one's need. Samuel Beckett says, "Try again, fail again, fail better." That's the best that human beings will ever be able to do. And, therefore, what you need is to be able to surrender, to become what Dostoevsky calls a holy fool. Everybody else is a fool on this ship of fools, but a certain kind of fool, the holy fool, is going to be him or her who has been through hell and high water, who has recognized how wretched they are and surrendered themselves to something bigger, has been motivated to want to bear witness to the suffering of others—just as in the latter part of *The Brothers Karamazov*. They're still wretched even as they're holy fools.

Now, Brother Robby would accept—well, we can let him speak for himself—but I think he would accept that Antinomian, Jansenist, Protestant version of things, but he was still bringing that rich Thomistic architecture.

George: Because we need rules.

West: But how would you respond? Am I being fair?

George: You're being fair. This is the difference that we come back to time and time again.

West: That's right. That's right.

George: If we argued this out, I would have to enter some caveats and Cornel would have some caveats. At the beginning, it would look like we're really on opposite places across a chasm, and we'd get a little closer. We wouldn't actually come into complete agreement or harmony, but of course I recognize, probably in a way that the Greeks didn't, the fallenness of human nature. But the question is just how total our depravity—a characterization of our fallen condition that is more common in Protestant than in Catholic parlance—really is. I think that's where we probably do have a difference. I think there's a Protestant sensibility or understanding that Cornel has of total depravity.

It was explained to me by my late professor at Swarthmore, Linwood Urban, who taught me medieval philosophy and philosophy of religion. And I don't know if he's accurate here, but he used to quote John Calvin as saying human beings are so bad, so fallen, so depraved, that "on the day of judgment, even the elect will be obnoxious in the sight of God." Now that is really *total* depravity and we have nothing we can go on of our own resources or our God-given reason or anything like that to get anywhere. Not even our good actions will redeem us. All we can do is surrender to God's grace.

Because I recognize fallenness. Unlike, say, Plato or Aristotle, I would say we need God's grace. Grace is an important factor for me as a Christian, but I would insist perhaps against Cornel, though he'd have to speak for himself here, that grace properly understood, perfects nature. It doesn't replace nature or abolish nature, or overcome it. So, we have our natural inclinations to the good. They are oftentimes blocked or hijacked by wayward desires, and our capitulation to wayward desires, our yielding to temptation. When St. Paul says, "the good that I would do I do not, and the evil that I would not do, I do," he's recognizing that we want to do good, we want to avoid evil, and yet we find ourselves yielding. And I don't think just on our own resources without God's grace, we're going to be able to overcome that. So, see, I'm entering the caveats now that are going to bring us closer.

West: Oh, absolutely. I mean when Kafka said in a conversation with his friend and biographer Max Brod there's hope for God, but no hope for us, he didn't have to read Calvin and Luther to get that. He's got his own tradition coming out of Jewish Kabbalistic sensibilities. Reading Kierkegaard, Kafka says that he's the only one who recognizes me. What he's saying in part is that Kafka does believe that art is a kind of prayer. So, he's got a conception of grace that allows him to keep going. But what grace does—it doesn't complete—it erupts.

You see, grace is an eruption of nature. This is from Karl Barth who was the greatest Protestant theologian of the twentieth century. Grace erupts and it creates this sudden interruption or conversion known as *metanoia*, a complete change of mind that comes with repentance and may involve a psychological crisis or breakdown. But if it's just completing, it's almost additive and complementary. It is not, oh no. Your whole world needs to turn upside down.

George: But you see the difference here between the Catholic and the Protestant sensibility and the Catholic and the Protestant understanding. And you can also see how it sounds in the beginning as though it is a vast chasm. As we push each other, as we enter our caveats and our distinctions and so forth, we don't end up in the same place. But it doesn't seem like an unbridgeable chasm anymore.

And here's where there's a genuine disagreement. We do have differences of opinion on what account should be given of, for example, our fallenness. We agree, man is fallen. We largely agree on what that means and what its consequences are and implications. We agree that it requires more than what we ourselves can provide. So, we need a redeemer. We need grace. But then when we get into the finer details, he's going to be quoting Barth, who's the archetypal Protestant, twentieth century neo-orthodox scholar, and my views will be much more in line with those of Karol Wojtyla, Pope John Paul II, or Joseph Ratzinger, Benedict XVI.

It seems that in an ideological age, hypocrisy is the one unforgivable sin. Thus, because Jefferson's writing "all men are created equal and endowed by their creator with certain unalienable rights" is not reconcilable with his ownership of slaves, this hypocrisy is said to invalidate not only his idea, but the legitimacy of the founding itself. How did this come about?

George: It used to be that hypocrisy was understood as the tribute that vice pays to virtue. I think that's the attitude we should have toward hypocrisy. It doesn't approve of it. It discourages it. It tries to prevent it, but it doesn't dismiss what's good, because the person who is advocating for the good falls short in his personal life, perhaps even profoundly.

Young people are often performing for each other to show how virtuous they are. They're performing for themselves to reassure themselves they're virtuous. That's because in this era of identity politics, we have come to identify virtue not with having a good personal character formed by the traditional virtues of fortitude, temperance, chastity, courage, and so forth, classical virtues, theological virtues such as faith, hope, and love. Rather we've identified virtue with having the correct opinions about things. To show, to "perform," for others having the "correct" opinions. And so, you find folks on campus vehemently condemning whoever is considered not woke, or not woke enough.

West: But it's the denial. When you have discourses of denial, you see people say, well, George Washington owned slaves and engaged in the Indian wars. Yes, but he's still a founding father. In that role he was heroic. And if you deny Washington and Jefferson these truths, then you're going to get a very one-sided critique. You're going to say, "No, take his statue down. Let's no longer invoke him." What do you mean? He actually engaged in a magnificent struggle against some of the most powerful forces of evil of his day, in the form of the British Empire. Now there are other forms of evil in his day that he was complicit with. But we don't say, My God, he's human. Instead, people have elevated him beyond the human and so the founding fathers are not subject to any Socratic reflection and critique. Then you're going to get the flip side of it. And, that's one of the things we try to talk about in class.

George: Absolutely right. Jefferson said two other things. Speaking specifically of slavery, he said, "I tremble for my country when I reflect that God is just, and that His justice will not sleep forever." But he also acknowledged that slavery was a deeply embedded institution in the culture and very hard to get rid of. "Slavery is like having a wolf by the ears. You know you cannot hold him, but you dare not let him go." I think for people like Jefferson, they didn't see a way out.

Jefferson himself was something of a spendthrift. Manumitting his slaves would have meant the destruction of his life essentially, or his way of life. It would have reduced him to poverty, but he should have done it anyway. It would have been a heroic act. Justice required him to manumit his slaves, but it would have had a devastating effect on his life.

We frail, fallen, fallible human beings will always fall short of our principles. But that doesn't mean that the principles are wrong or bad, nor does it mean that we shouldn't try our best to live up to them individually and collectively.

Now, it's not our job, not the job of any professor, to tell our students what to think, including whether America is fundamentally a good country or not. At least, that's my view of the vocation of teaching. It is my job to make sure my students understand the principles of the American founding, the principles of the Declaration of Independence and the Constitution. It's also my job to help them to assess critically, over history and now, the extent to which we have or haven't lived up to those principles.

Now as it happens, I do believe that our principles are sound, and good, and true. I believe that the Declaration and the Constitution reflect the principle of the profound, inherent, and equal dignity of each human being. I believe they are principles of the sort you would choose if you really did believe that human beings, every single human being, is made in the image and likeness of God. And I believe that when students understand those principles, when they truly understand them, they will see that they are good and true.

But it's not my job to get them to make that normative judgment. It's my job to get them to understand the principles. Then it's their job to judge for themselves whether they are good, and right, and true. But now, speaking as a citizen and not just a teacher, and as one who does believe that their truth will shine forth, I think it's an urgent task of our schools, colleges, and universities to restore civic education to the forefront of their mission. Because if we do that, and students truly understand our principles, they will affirm them, and will more likely resolve in their own minds to do what they can to help this country live up to its principles, and not reject it root and branch. They won't become enemies of patriotism, but true patriots whose patriotism is evident in their desire for the country to be more fully in harmony with its principles.

West: For me, because I tried to engage in a fundamental quest for truth, and beauty, and goodness, and all that—for me, a fundamental truth of human history is the way in which hatred, and greed, and envy, and resentment, and various forms of domination and exploitation are dominant institutional practices. And American history is part of human history. The philosopher Walter Benjamin was right in his essay "On the Concept of History": We don't know of an empire, a nation-state, a centralized form of power not connected in some way to forms of barbarism. If somehow America could create a colonial settlement on Indigenous people's land, without being connected to any form of barbarism, let's see the evidence. If you can't get your economy off the ground without creating a slave economy, or Black folk not being able to vote until 1965—no matter what the principles were on paper—then what are we talking about?

But that's not a unique failing of America. It's part of human history. You see it in Africa, you see it in Asia, you see it in Latin America, you see it among Indigenous peoples, you see it in Europe. We're just telling folks, "Look, let's be adults about this thing. Let's be truthful about it." History is not a pretty picture. No matter what people say about America and so forth, settler colonial projects have higher possibilities. They may have very ugly undersides, but the same is true inside our own souls. The same is true in every community. The same is true for every church, mosque, synagogue, or temple. Let's just be candid and honest about this. But then they say, "Well, it's going to trigger me that I have to read about the lynching." I understand. I've had folk in my family who were lynched, too. But we have to come to terms with the realities.

George: Right.

West: You come to terms with the realities. Various people have their realities; the Irish have theirs, and the Jews have theirs, and the southern Italians have theirs, and the Ethiopians have theirs. This is what it is to be part of human history, you see? People say, "Well, I want America to be a good country." The best of America is good, and the worst of America is barbaric and hateful and greed-ridden, like any other history in that regard. Do you say, "Well, I hate America." Okay, but do you hate humanity itself? Do you hate yourself for being human? "Well, I wouldn't go that far." Then let's draw some distinctions here. Or, they may say, "I am consistent. I hate humanity."

I had some brothers come up to me after a lecture at Columbia saying, "You know, Brother West, I just can't wait until the extinction of the human race takes place. Because look what we've done to the planet. Look what we've done to each other." And I said, yes, it's true. We human beings revel in gratuitous violence in a way that elephants don't, even lions and tigers don't. Yes, that's who we are as human beings. Dostoevsky got it right. It's that ugly. It's that vicious. It's that grim. But is that all?

Then they say, "Oh brother, well, you're still romantic. You're looking for something more?" No, I'm not looking for something more. Look in the history. You still see joy. You still see struggles for equality. You still see ecstasy. You still see community. You still see forms of solidarity, going against the grain. Yes. That's what the evidence is. You've still got decent folk out there. You've got people of integrity out there. They're not a mass movement, never have been, never will be.

But that just means you fortify yourself even more. You bear witness even stronger. You tell your truths more courageously, and bear the cost even more willingly, because you want to be one of the extensions of this great tradition, going back to Socrates, and Jesus, go back to Cicero with a dose of Spartacus thrown in, or to Harriet Tubman's courageous witness. You see?

George: What Cornel is saying—just to take it down to its skeleton—is that when we're teaching students about America, and American history, our responsibility is to tell the truth, full stop. The whole truth, which is a complicated truth—

West: Given our fallibility.

George: Yep—and nothing but the truth. That's it. Tell them the truth. Tell them the whole truth, warts and all. But these days, of course, you also have to remind them of the good things.

West: Oh, yes.

George: Because they want to focus so much on the bad things that they lose sight of what Cornel was talking about, the solidarity, the movements for equality, the joy. Then nothing but the truth. Don't spice it up with something that will turn it into a just-so story.

West: Yes.

George: You just let the truth come out in its fullness and then let—trust—them to take it from there.

West: Then you ask, how do you account for yourself? You are as American as Martin Luther King Jr., the Ku Klux Klan, baseball, and apple pie. You think you are the first American to come forward with this indictment? Please, you're not reinventing the wheel. Who do you think Lydia Maria Child was, a white woman who wrote the preface to the various slave narratives? Who do you think Elijah Lovejoy was, a graduate of Princeton Theological Seminary, who got killed in Missouri as a white abolitionist? Who do you think William Lloyd Garrison was? Who do you think Paul Sweezy and Stanley Aronowitz were? Who do you think Jeff Stout and Paul Bove are? Who do you think Harry Magdoff was? Who do you think Ella Baker or Harry Belafonte were? They were Americans too, just like you.

Now, they didn't always triumph. And you might not triumph either. But you keep at it. You don't know. History is unpredictable. But they left a witness. A beautiful witness.

Chapter Six

Discerning Truth Today: Abortion, Race, Identity

You have said that young people come to you with convictions already formed. And you affirm that you are not relativists, you believe there are right answers. But young people—and frankly most others—are never going to get to a depth where their convictions are founded in ultimate truth. Our convictions are always going to be products of our experience, our communities, the dominant ideas of our time. How deep can you go with young people? What's your role here?

Robert P. George: Our role as teachers is to unsettle our students. Cornel's absolutely right when he introduces our classes sometimes by saying, "The whole point of the education you are receiving here at Princeton and in this classroom is to unsettle you."

I sometimes startle my students by opening with the following line, "This is America, right?" "Right," everybody says. "And in America, we're free." "Right, yeah we're free." "And as Americans we're entitled to our opinions, right?" They say, "Right." And then I say, "No, you are not. Not in this classroom." And they're shocked: Professor George is going to impose his conservative opinions on us? Professor George must be a hypocrite because he's out there strongly advocating for freedom of speech and civil liberties, and yet he's just told us that we're not entitled to our opinions?

And then I explain: No, in this classroom, you're not entitled to your opinions unless you earn the right to them. How do you do that? By *thinking*, by *reasoning your way to your opinions*. I'm not interested in your opinions if you're just emoting, if you are just vocalizing feelings that have no rational basis. But I'm very interested in your opinions when they are the fruit of reflection, deliberation, and judgment. When you are willing and able to give reasons, make arguments, marshal evidence for your views. Then God bless you, it doesn't matter whether I agree with you or not. You are entitled to your opinions and by expressing them, you make an important contribution in this class. It's not whether you agree or disagree with me that matters. It's whether you are willing to reason yourself to your opinions.

Cornel West: What makes Robby not just a masterful teacher, but someone whose integrity people acknowledge, even when they might have a deep hostility toward certain political stances he has on abortion, same-sex marriage, or whatever, is the example he sets that the students can see in the classroom, an example that fellow citizens acknowledge in relating to him as a human being and a thinker. And that example is not reducible in any way to his particular judgments, opinions, or ideology or politics or even religion.

George: Many people today will say something like, "By challenging my views or the way I choose to live or things that I do, you are denying my humanity. You are erasing me." Now, it's only possible to make that error if you have identified yourself, your very self, with your feelings so tightly that you have placed them beyond criticism. If you regard your feelings as central to your identity, where they are determining your views on moral and political issues, then any challenge to your political views or your moral beliefs or your practices or your lifestyle will be interpreted by you as a personal attack. Because we wrap our emotions so tightly around our convictions, we identify our very selves with them. There's always the danger—and it's heightened in an age of identity politics—that we lack sufficient detachment to be able to receive criticism without interpreting the criticism as the equivalent of a physical attack.

Anything anybody says to challenge your views, even politely, sincerely, earnestly, even if it's out of a regard for you and your well-being, you will necessarily interpret as a personal attack, an assault on your personhood. I think it's important to have convictions. Cornel and I both certainly have them, and we're prepared to defend them and act on them. Cornel's prepared to go to jail for them. I hope if it came to it that I would be willing to do that.

West: He's willing to bail me out.

George: (*Laughs*) That's true. So, I believe it's very important for us to be people of conviction, but we need at every moment a certain distance from our convictions. To leave the room, we need to be open to the possibility that we might be wrong, to pay due respect to our own fallibility, to acknowledge our inadequacy, to the fact that we're never going to get the truth fully.

West: Not fully.

George: And even if we do get part of it, we're not going to have the whole of it. We need that distance from our convictions that will allow us to be people of intellectual humility as well as conviction. And to be people who can learn and change our convictions under the weight of reason and argument and evidence, when the responsible thing is to shift what we think and believe.

Too often in heated public debates we depict our side as the good guys and the other as the bad guys. We assume that all the good faith and goodwill is on our side. Everybody on the other side is a person of bad faith and bad will. We assume that there are no valid considerations motivating people on the other side. And that's just wrong. This means that we can't simply say that the other side is just straightforwardly mistaken.

Let's focus on some of those tougher questions, where it appears there is truth on both sides. Take abortion. It is true that a woman, in our view, is the owner of her body and has certain inalienable rights. At the same time, we must acknowledge that the fetus from gestation will, if not interrupted, eventuate in a human being with moral, legal, and political rights. At what point do we cut those rights short? Are we denying one truth or the other, when we are forced to make a choice?

George: Well, the first point I would make here is a rather bloodless one, and that is that the principle of non-contradiction holds. Something cannot both be and not be in the same respect at the same time, which means we can't resolve an issue like this or any of the other issues that you might have in mind, simply by saying what this side says is completely true, and what that side says is also completely true. That can't be the case, because the law of non-contradiction forbids that. But here's what we can say and what we should say and what is too rarely said. Often enough people on both sides of hotly contested issues can and should acknowledge the good faith and goodwill of those who hold different convictions. It is not contradicting the principle of non-contradiction to recognize that there are valid concerns on both sides.

I'm coming at this from the point of view of a pro-life person. Women's dignity is important. Women's autonomy is important. There are many ways, historically, and even today, in which women's dignity has been denied and women's autonomy has been unjustly limited. Pregnancy can be very difficult and there can be dangerous circumstances that being pregnant puts a woman in. And those challenges and dangers to a fellow human being—someone no less made in the image and likeness of God than you or I—have got to be addressed. The whole question is this: Is the way to address them by permitting the destruction of the child in the womb? Now, I say "child in the womb," already making a judgment as to the status of the fetus.

In my own case, the Catholic understanding has always been that you may perform an act that would result in the death of a child in the womb where it was necessary to preserve the mother's life and the death of the child would be a side effect of performing an act that you would otherwise perform, like removing a cancerous uterus, despite the fact that there's a baby there. So, in the Catholic understanding, the principle gives no priority to either mother or child as such. Both are of equal dignity. But you can perform an act that will result in fetal death if the *object* is not to bring about the death of the fetus, but rather to save the life of the mother by, for example, removing an embryo that is attached to the fallopian tube in an ectopic pregnancy.

The Catholic version looks a little different from the traditional Jewish version, which I think is very interesting. So, if you look at the writings of strongly pro-life Jewish authorities like Rabbi David Novak, the scholar of Jewish law and ethics at the University of Toronto, he accounts for the Jewish position, that where you have to make a choice, you are obligated, not just allowed, but obligated to save the mother's life, in the following way. Rabbi Novak says that the ground or foundation for the judgment is in the proximity of the mother's life. The mother's life is more proximate to us. And he adds that, typically, a woman would have other children that would need to be taken care of.

So, although you cannot perform an abortion under traditional Jewish law, as Rabbi Novak interprets it, for the sake of getting rid of an unwanted child in the situation where the life of the mother is not threatened, there are good reasons to choose the mother's life even if the result is the death of the child. The Catholic position doesn't require you to give priority to one over the other. The act can be performed even if it results in fetal death, so long as that's not the object of the act. That's sometimes called the principle of double effect. By the same token, if a woman decides that she would prefer to sacrifice her own life to make sure the child survives or to maximize the odds of its survival, that would not be considered a suicide or an unethical act, as it may well be in Judaism if Rabbi Novak's position is true. But look at how narrow the difference is. It's a very, very, very narrow difference that would apply to a fraction of cases.

But before getting into any of that, it's incumbent on me to make that case, on behalf of the child in the womb and his or her inherent equal dignity. And number two, even if I can successfully make that case, which I believe I can, that does not erase the valid concerns that are motivating people on the other side. So, while I would not accept their conclusion, having been persuaded that the destruction of the child is an unjust attack on an innocent human being, it is again incumbent upon me and people on my side to join with people on the other side in finding ways to address, to the extent that we can, by non-lethal means, the legitimate concerns that people have and the problems that really do exist for women who find themselves pregnant in circumstances that make that very, very difficult for them. Does that make sense?

West: That makes a whole lot of sense. I just like, again, the way you started and acknowledged this sense of good faith. And not just on two sides, but on a variety of different sides, because we're talking about multiplicity; we're talking about different perspectives, different lenses through which people are looking at the world. And to me, that's crucial, because you see, part of the distrust that breaks down the dialogue in regard to abortion or same-sex marriage or whatever, is that people feel as if their valid concerns are being discarded.

There are historical realities that one must come to terms with. They don't determine the conclusion in the debate, but they do set the background conditions that can undercut any trust that allowed a debate to proceed the way in which Robby just laid it out so beautifully. The same would be true in terms of the focus on the child.

Now, Robby, in a way, is very different from many brothers and sisters on the conservative side because he's concerned about the child in the womb. He's concerned about the child in the ghetto, in the hood, in the barrio, and on the reservation. If we hear people making a claim about how they're deeply concerned about the child and don't say a mumbling word about child poverty—don't say a mumbling word about children's access to opportunities once they're born—then people figure, well, maybe there was this concern really about just the woman. Where's the concern about the child after they're out of the womb? Robby happens to be an abolitionist in terms of alleviating poverty using market mechanisms a little bit more than I would, of course. But he's definitely concerned about the child over time.

If people feel as if there's all this talk about the child and no talk about child poverty, that reinforces a distrust. And you say, "Oh, no, this is just a clash of ideologies. This is not a Socratic dialogue at all." You say, "No, there's genuine moral compassion for the child, on the conservative side." We can debate; when does the child become a person with the rights you're talking about, with the dignity and sanctity that must be acknowledged? That's a valid concern. And simply so, in terms of the women, not just the woman's body, but also acknowledging that they're in circumstances and conditions under which, once they do have the baby, everything could collapse and therefore they want to have an abortion to be able to live a certain life, and allow flourishing to take place in their life. That's a valid concern, too.

George: I would just add that I think it's a terrible shame that this particular issue eventually came to divide Americans along ideological lines. It was not like that from the beginning. For most of our history, abortion was not a political issue. There was a consensus that it was wrong and should not be permitted, except in the circumstances where there was a genuine threat to the mother's life.

When abortion became an issue in the 1960s, it did not divide people along ideological lines. There were very, very prominent progressives who were pro-life. There were prominent conservatives who wanted to liberalize abortion laws. It was only in the 1980s that it became a mark of being a liberal or a progressive to be pro-choice, and the mark of a conservative to be pro-life. And that's a purely contingent fact. There's nothing in the logic of the debate that requires a person to be on one side or the other, depending on whether you're a Democrat or Republican, a progressive or a conservative.

Being pro-life myself, I regret very much that it's now considered a conservative position, even though I regard myself as a conservative, because I miss the contributions that were made to the pro-life cause in the early phase of the movement by notable progressives, like Nat Hentoff, or Jesse Jackson, early in his career before he decided to run for president. By then, the issue had started to become partisan, and he, with no explanation, simply switched his position because, politically, he had no choice but to do that if he was going to seek the Democratic nomination. Up to that point, he had been a very vocal defender of the pro-life cause. Governor Robert P. Casey, the late governor of Pennsylvania, is another. There were many, many prominent pro-life progressives, and I want them back. I don't want the pro-life movement to be a partisan, Republican, or conservative thing. I'm willing to have partisan, conservative-liberal debates about a lot of things, but I'm really unhappy that this one has become a partisan ideological debate because there's no need for it to be.

I also think it's worth pointing out that the majority of people in the pro-life movement are female, not male. There are millions and millions of American women who are pro-life. So, the movement can't be written off as "anti-woman." To do that, you would have to deny either that Fannie Lou Hamer was pro-life, which, of course, she very vocally was, or that Fannie Lou Hamer was a woman. You're going to have to say that Mildred Jefferson, the first African-American woman to graduate from Harvard Medical School, was somehow anti-woman because she served three terms as president of the National Right to Life movement. The failure to acknowledge the fact, lay aside all the ethical questions, just the sheer fact that women no less than men are divided on this issue, is a problem.

West: This is again where these two different registers overlap, but they're not identical. Not just in America, but the history of patriarchy overall is one in which the value of a woman's life did not have the same status as a man's. That's the historical record. It cannot be denied. And somehow, we've got to be able to acknowledge that truth and still acknowledge the truth that Robby's talking about, in terms of how complicated this issue is, in which women's voices are heard on both sides.

George: The nineteenth-century feminists, the founding mothers of feminism, at least the leadership class of the founding mothers—and I strongly suspect it was the whole body—were strongly pro-life. Susan B. Anthony, Alice Paul, figure after figure, to the extent that they said anything about abortion at all, were on the pro-life side, seeing abortion not as something valuable for women, but as something that let men off the hook. They understood that the problem was patriarchy. Cornel just put his finger on the devaluing of the life of a woman. But the nineteenth-century feminists didn't see the solution the way Simone de Beauvoir, Gloria Steinem, or other second wave feminists, saw the issue.

They saw it the reverse of the way the first generation, the founding mothers of feminism, saw it. And to this day, I would make the case that the real beneficiaries of the abortion license are men who can escape responsibility for children that they are responsible for, by saying, "It's the woman's choice, not my problem." Maybe you can force him by law to pay child support if the woman decides to have the child. But the man will say, "I contest the right of the law to do that. She made the decision to keep the baby. I wanted the abortion. I was even willing to pay for it. Therefore, I shouldn't be financially responsible for that child."

West: And that's part of the history of patriarchy. Men's voices have been the dominant ones in determining abortion policy up until the 1960s, right? The very tradition that Brother Robby and I are critically appropriating—Athens to Jerusalem to Rome—is shot through with patriarchy, shot through with slavery, shot through with class domination. That doesn't mean that tradition somehow is to be discarded or dismissed or somehow there aren't treasures therein. But if we're going to be committed to truth, then we're going to be committed to the truth of the very tradition that we are committed to in all of its various forms and voices and so forth.

George: And it's only the resources of that tradition you'd use to critique it.

West: We know Aristotle was a patriarchal thinker. That doesn't mean that the riches of his philosophical worldview are worthless. Now, Sappho, of course, is a counter-voice in that regard.

But the same would be true all the way up to the modern period. The same would be true in the American legal system and so forth, the slavery, the patriarchy, the class bias and so forth. It's all there.

George: But we're always going back for the critique to the principle of the profound and inherent and equal dignity of each and every member of the human family. And we have this principle in the West because chapter one of the very first book of the Hebrew Bible says that each and every human being is made in the image and likeness of God. So, where we see injustice, whether it's in the form of patriarchy or in the form of slavery, we can have a critical perspective on it, because it conflicts with our fundamental belief in the profound inherent and equal dignity of each and every member of the human family. And the one thing we always have to avoid is trying to solve an injustice by introducing a practice which itself runs afoul of the principle of equal dignity.

West: But then, at the same time though, you've got Antisthenes, a great student of Socrates, who calls into question the Greek-barbarian distinction—

George: Oh, this is true.

West: You've got Stoics like Epictetus, you've got pagans who are calling for the dignity of each and every person independent of our biblical scriptures, that resonates and has elective affinities and deep similarities with our Judeo-Christian sensibility.

George: We do, and that's what we call the natural law tradition. These pre-Christian thinkers were able to understand, on the basis of unaided reason, and without the assistance of the data of revelation, the fundamental truth of human dignity. Now, some of our early Christian fathers suspected that Plato either had some secret access to the Hebrew scripture or was given some equivalent revelation as a way of explaining how he could know certain things that seemed to be distinctive biblical contributions. But I don't think any of the church fathers ultimately came down in favor of that belief.

West: It's stretching things. It reminds me of the Yiddish writers who used to say as a joke—but also with a certain seriousness—that Chekhov must have been Yiddish, because nobody else could have such a profound comic sensibility. The beauty and sorrow of people with no land, only a language and general history. What a compliment to Chekhov. But no, Chekhov wasn't a Yiddish brother. He is Russian. And you simply have to say, "No, people make their own ways and may end up in very similar places."

I'm saying that because there's a number of ways to get to certain consequences of the *Imago Dei*. I don't want to argue that we Christians have the only gateway to it. It's there in Hebrew scripture in a profound way—with unbelievable consequences and ramifications and repercussions down through time and space to the present day.

George: What Aquinas says is that revelation can profoundly illuminate what we can see, albeit through a glass darkly, by the light of natural reason, the inferior, but nevertheless, real light of natural reason.

The two of you have very different views of the Israel–Palestine conflict and you must have discussed this topic many times over the years. Given the divisive demonstrations in the streets and on college campuses this spring over the war in Gaza, it seems likely you will have to deal with these divisions in the classroom. What do you think is the best way to engage these issues that are driven by such passionate moral commitments?

West: I would begin with the notion that we are a wretched species—although we're also wonderful—and so we ought never be surprised when we see highly concentrated forms of hatred and violence and contempt for each other. I was just thinking about *Antigone*, in one of those great choruses, where the play talks about how wretched and wonderful we are simultaneously. Of course, you get the same thing in the Hebrew scriptures and in the Christian and Islamic traditions too. But I would begin with that, because I don't want young people to be so obsessed with the present that they become overwhelmed with human wretchedness. That so often leads to a narrow, Manichaean view of the world in which they have to cleanse themselves, purify themselves, put themselves on the side of light, and put so many others on the side of darkness.

One of the worst things we human beings have done over time is to respond to overwhelming evil, organized greed, institutionalized hatred, or routinized indifference toward the vulnerable by attempting to put ourselves in some saintly space, as if we're not tainted with some of what we're actually against. The question becomes this: How do we come to terms with the civil war taking place on the battlefield of our own souls? And then how do we attempt to make the kind of wise and courageous judgments that

shun Manichaean views of the world, and worse, cynical, nihilistic views of the world in which nothing matters whatsoever,
other than who has the power?

Why do you think this particular conflict, with all the
wars and genocides going on in the world, has stirred
up so much passion among young people?

West: I think there are two reasons. One is that this is so much
an American affair because of the American support for Israel—
militarily, financially, ideologically. And it is an American affair
in which, as on so many other fronts, the face of American
hypocrisy and mendacity has been ripped off, and people see
criminality and barbarity so that America in general loses its
claim to innocence. And for the younger generation, which has
been socialized in a certain way to this innocence, all of a sudden they see violence beneath the innocence when, for example, you get somebody like Joe Biden saying that we've held
our investigation and we don't see any violation of international
law or human rights. America is presenting itself as exemplar of
upholding international law and human rights, and when the
young generation looks at this, they can only say, "That's a lie,
Mr. Biden." Do we really believe a precious Palestinian baby has
the same value as a precious Israeli baby? I definitely do!

The second thing, of course, has to do with the very, very
complicated, delicate, and difficult role of Jewish brothers
and sisters in the history of the West (and you could say of
the species). People find it just so difficult to conceive of the
notion that a Jewish people who have been so thoroughly hated

for 2,500 years, terrorized for 2,500 years, and traumatized for 2,500 years can be human and can therefore hate, terrorize, and traumatize others. And how do you not fall into any kind of anti-hate, anti-Jewish, or anti-human pitfall to come to terms with the humanity even of the 2,500-year victims of inhumanity?

Here again, this shows the ways in which human beings, no matter who they are, make choices—moral, spiritual, and political—not based on just their past, but on how they've been shaped and how they proceed. And of course, you've got the deep, deep divide within not just American Jewry, but world Jewry, between the younger generations, so often now tilted toward joining the encampments and joining the various struggles against the Israeli occupation and many members of, if not most of, their parents' and grandparents' generations.

There's clearly a powerful claim to truth on both sides of this conflict. Robby, in a classroom context, how would you engage this issue, which can lead, as Cornel said, to a Manichaean desire to be pure, and to project all the evil, perhaps the evil in oneself, onto somebody else.

George: The first thing we have to think about is this: What is our fundamental mission? What is our fundamental vocation as teachers, especially as university teachers? It is to shape the young men and women entrusted to our care, those we are supposed to educate, and to form them to be determined truth seekers, courageous truth speakers, and lifelong learners. When we lay that foundation, we immediately see the wisdom and the truth in what otherwise just strikes us as a cliché. Our task as teachers is not to tell students what to think, but to empower them, encourage them, and enable them to think more deeply, more critically (including self-critically), and to think for themselves.

If we are talking about a dispute like the Israel–Palestine dispute, the one thing we know is that students are going to come into class with opinions. They are not coming from nowhere. Some students will be in a position where they haven't really formed their views. They have a sense that there are some arguments on one side and some on the other side, but they have not formed a firm position. But a lot of students will come in with a very firm position, and very often that position will be more tribal than thought-out.

By tribal I don't mean fundamentally Israeli as opposed to Palestinian, or vice-versa. What more often calls the tune for our students—not in every case, obviously—is ideological tribalism. Our task as teachers is to break that way of thinking because it's not thinking. Tribalism impedes thinking. Our job is to get our students to think—again, not to tell them what to think. My job is not to get my students to think the way I do about the Middle East. Cornel doesn't see his job as getting his students to think the way he thinks about the Middle East. Both of us, whether we're teaching together or teaching separately, understand that our job is to help our students to think for themselves in a very deep and critical—including self-critical—way.

I want to lay some emphasis on the term "self-criticism." When people have a tribal mindset, the last thing they want to consider are the best arguments on the competing sides. When they have a narrative, they want to stick to it and shout it at the other guy. They do not want to consider what the other guy has to say. We are vulnerable, and we often don't want to take the risk of questioning ideas that we regard as so central to our identity. We are tribal by nature, and we do not want to say or do anything that would alienate us from our tribe because we need its support. But if we're going to be thinkers—not just tribalists, not just ideologues, not just dogmatists—then we are going to have to hear what the other side says.

My sense of what we need to do in the classroom is to expose students to the considerations and the arguments that give some plausibility—and sometimes validity—to claims on the other side. In both my case and Cornel's, students are not in any doubt about where we stand, and that's fine. What we have to make clear to them is that we don't desire nor tolerate them simply spitting our views back at us. If that's what is happening in the classroom, then we are failing. We have to make sure that they are genuinely thinking, thinking for themselves, and thinking in a self-critical way. That's hard, but it's our job.

*Let's talk about Aaron Bushnell, who set himself on fire
to protest what he called genocide in Gaza. Cornel has
praised the young man's moral courage and conviction
and referred to him as a martyr for truth and justice.
Robby has tended to lament and deplore this action,
regarding it more as a symptom of mental or emotional
disturbance. Can you address these differing views?*

West: I thought of Cato the Younger and the significance of killing oneself as a political act; under what circumstances does that go hand in hand with a certain kind of moral courage and moral witness? I also thought of the Vietnamese monk who famously immolated himself to protest the Vietnam War. On a personal level, I was very moved by what this brother did because so many people who are involved in various forms of protest feel a sense of impotence and powerlessness—not just frustration. I was very moved in that sense. But there's always the danger of self-indulgence. There's a danger of self-righteousness. There's a danger of acting as if this is an act of purity. I don't believe in purity at all, even when you kill yourself, even when you decide to live, even when you join an encampment, even when you oppose the encampment. These are human beings. Across the board. And the fundamental question is: How do you acknowledge that however deep our disagreements are, those are human beings on the other side? How do you retain some compassionate attachment to their humanity, even given their disagreement?

In the case of this particular brother who reached the end of his rope, as it were, and engaged in this kind of action, I was deeply moved by it. Now it's true—Cato the Younger, the Vietnamese monk, or even Africans jumping off of slave ships—I don't really know the states of their psyches. If we do have evidence that he didn't have both paddles in the water, then that becomes an added factor. But I want to push Brother Robby and ask if we have some evidence that there was some psychological instability here. That would add a factor that I would have to come to terms with.

George: The principle that we ought to be willing to be self-sacrificial in serving the causes we believe in is a principle that I affirm; at the same time, however, I very strongly affirm the principle of the basic sanctity of human life. And, for someone like me who affirms that principle, it is never morally acceptable, it is always wrong, and gravely so, to intend death, whether the death of another person or one's own death, whether one intends one's death as an end in itself or as a means to some other end.

That does not entail a pacifist position. For reasons that are very well-articulated in the long tradition that's sometimes called "just war" theory, going all the way back to Saint Augustine and Thomas Aquinas, that principle means that while you should be willing to accept death, if necessary, for a great cause, you may not intend death, including your own. That's a violation of the very principle that Mr. Bushnell himself wanted to stand up for—the principle that innocent people should not be killed.

But I cannot justify suicide, even for the sake of advancing a political cause. I also am concerned that if we do not make clear that killing oneself is unacceptable, we're just going to get more of it. When you glamorize something, it will tempt people, especially those who are not emotionally strong or stable. If they see that somebody gets a lot of favorable attention and is regarded as a martyr, other people will desire that treatment. That's why, when Aaron Bushnell performed this act, I said I don't think we should be glorifying this because I don't want this to happen to somebody else's son, daughter, grandson, granddaughter, husband, boyfriend, or anyone, for that matter.

West: Yes, but you would accept the distinction between being deeply moved by a certain kind of moral and spiritual witness such that you are willing to pay the ultimate price. I would never want to use the language of glorification but instead that of being deeply moved by a certain kind of witness. I'm deeply moved by a Martin Luther King Jr. or Fannie Lou Hamer, who spoke out in a white supremacist society, predicated on such hatred and contempt for black folk. You know that when you say certain things, you basically are committing a kind of suicide. I would never glorify that, but I'm deeply moved by the kind of moral character and sense of virtue that goes into the depth of one's commitment to do something that leads toward a killing of oneself implicitly, explicitly, directly, or indirectly. Would you accept that distinction, my brother?

George: I certainly understand and share the belief that the willingness to sacrifice oneself for a cause that one believes in is in itself a noble thing. But I would want to stop short of saying anything that would encourage anyone to take his own life. But I should make a distinction. I would encourage someone to, say, take a stand in defense of innocent people, knowing that as a result he was going to be in the line of fire and possibly get killed. In the latter case, one is not intending death. One is accepting death as a side effect of standing up for something one believes in. I think what Brother Bushnell did was intend his own death. And that's where I would draw the line, and why I would not want to say anything that would encourage somebody else's son or daughter, granddaughter, grandson to do that.

West: Yes, yes. Was it John Donne who wrote that text on God's suicide on the cross? What do you think of this notion of the cross itself as a site of divine suicide?

George: This was rejected as an understanding of the crucifixion and the mission of Jesus by the church from the very beginning. It was speculated on: How do you distinguish Jesus's willingness to accept death, given that as the Son of God, he could have avoided it? Does that mean he intended it? And of course, the answer that the church has given across all Christian traditions is that Jesus accepted death at the hands of someone else who willed it. He did not himself will his death.

Remember how he was taunted by one thief on one side of him? And how the thief crucified on the other side verbally reached out to him? The thief who taunted him says, "If you are Christ, save yourself and us." And of course, Jesus doesn't do that. And in that way, he accepts death as a saving act. The other thief doesn't join in and tells the first to stop taunting Jesus. And then he says, "Lord, remember me when you come into your kingdom." And then Jesus gives a gift that no one else in the whole history of the human race has ever received when he says to the so-called good thief, "On this very day you will be with me in Paradise."

West: Do I remember that? Absolutely. Because again, it is a question of being profoundly moved by someone who was willing to lay down his life. When Jesus said that he who is willing to lay down his life for a friend is manifesting the highest form of love—or one of the highest forms—that's what I'm trying to zero in on.

George: Let's contrast two cases, and let me see if this makes sense to you. Remember that very brave young man who stood in front of the tank in Tiananmen Square in China?

West: Absolutely.

George: Had that tank run over him and killed him, would we have said he committed suicide? I want to say no. We would have said he was murdered. Now, I see that the impulse of Aaron Bushnell is similar: it's a self-sacrificial act. In that respect, the two are the same. But in Bushnell's case, somebody didn't murder him. He killed himself, what used to be called self-murder. That's the principle I want to maintain: that for the sake of protecting the sanctity of human life, we must never intend death. That means whether it is someone else's or our own, either as an end in itself, because you hate somebody, or because you're trying to get somebody else to do what you want.

West: But we're still deeply moved in both cases where human beings, out of great courage and commitment, are willing to pay the ultimate price in the face of an ugly form of oppression and domination.

George: The self-sacrificial element is what the two have in common.

West: Exactly.

George: But I think they're of a completely different moral standing. That's my own view.

Robby's concern was that an action such as this would negatively affect those who might be mentally or emotionally unstable. But there is also the question of whether it inflames more passion or hatred in ordinary people. This is an issue that has come up a lot. It seems like the temper of activism today arouses more negative passions in the general public. What do you think about the effects of these gestures—obstructing traffic or defacing works of art—in contrast to the Civil Rights movement which, while impassioned, was on the whole more tempered?

West: The effects intended and the unintended consequences are always multivariate. You have no real sense of them and no control over them. One effect could be a broader awakening of people who had not paid any attention to the issue at all. I think about that in terms of the Buddhist monk in the 1960s. You had a lot of folk who hadn't really paid that much attention, until all of a sudden you get this major act where people have to ask themselves: Where do I stand? How I define myself in relation to these issues? That to me is a positive thing. That's a way of shaking people who are sleepwalking. I think of Henry David Thoreau going to jail for not paying the poll tax. He was trying to shake a sleepwalking country in the face of the Mexican War that he thought was wrong, and facing down slavery, and so on. So that would be one effect.

When I think of the civil rights movement in the '60s, that was a very distinctive moment because there was such predominant moral and spiritual leadership from the very beginning. It was not just Rosa Parks and not just Martin Luther King Jr. How did Emmett Till's mother, at the funeral of her child who was only fourteen years old, step up in front of the world and say, "I don't have a minute to hate, I will pursue justice for the rest of my life"? That's the moral and spiritual greatness that the civil rights movement was able almost to take for granted early on. Martin Luther King Jr., Fannie Lou Hamer, and Medgar Evers all came out of this great tradition of black folk who refused to hate in the face of hatred, refused to counter-terrorize and just kill others when they were killed, refused to form black versions of the Ku Klux Klan when the Klan came at them, and refused to be wounded hurters, deciding instead to be wounded healers when they were traumatized. But that moral and spiritual greatness that the black freedom movement had in the '60s for the most part has been lost. That's part of the deep spiritual decay in the American empire. It's not just on the vanilla side of town; it's on the chocolate side too. Some of us are trying to keep that legacy alive. But it's very difficult because so much of the makings of it have been shattered by a whole host of things—commodification, narcissism, hedonism—and a whole lot of other things.

One thing I do want to point out is that when we look further back in history, what has been going on in the last few months is tame compared to what has come before. Thank God we haven't reached the point where we see massive killings and assassinations of leaders. It's one thing to shut down a bridge, and it's another thing to have major leaders of various organizations and parties shot down like dogs. We haven't had that. We even see this in American history. We have a history of violence that spills over at the highest levels. Thank God we haven't had that yet here. Of course, what we do have is not in any way something to brag about. Once you lose your moral and spiritual moorings, no matter what your issue is, you just find yourself falling into cycles of violence, hatred, and contempt.

George: A point on which Cornel and I deeply agree is that the model provided by figures such as Martin Luther King Jr. and Fannie Lou Hamer is the correct model when it comes to direct action: to try to rectify what one judges to be an injustice. Let's look at King in particular. Civil disobedience by definition is not legally justified. Civil disobedience means you are breaking the law. The question is, can it be morally justified? I agree with Cornel and with Dr. King that it can be, though it isn't always, but it can be morally justified when you're fighting against a great evil. Lawbreaking can be, in some circumstances, a morally legitimate thing to do. But as King himself pointed out, there are some conditions for that.

Number one, the lawbreaking cannot itself involve injustice to other people, meaning putting other people in unreasonable danger. It can't involve the violation of the rights of other people. And beyond that, as King pointed out, if one engages in civil disobedience, then part of what one is responsible for doing is accepting for oneself the consequences of that disobedience. King said that if you're going to do it, as he himself did, landing in Birmingham Jail, it's got to be done lovingly. Not with malice, not with hatred, not with any injustice to other people. Number two, it has to be done openly. You can't break the law secretly; you can't try to get away with it. You have to do it openly, so that other people can see you, and you'll be arrested (Cornel himself has done this many times). And number three, it's got to be done with a willingness to accept the consequences.

King did something else that I think is very important. He taught us by example, not just by precept. He provided a detailed justification for his actions, in which he engaged the counterarguments of people who criticized him. That letter from Birmingham Jail was not written to a bunch of racists. Quite the contrary. If you read the letter, you'll see him praising one of the eight clergymen to whom the letter was addressed—his critics—for the great witness to racial justice he had provided when he defied the segregation of his church and insisted on welcoming black families. I think that's the model. If you're going to do it, you have to do it in a way that doesn't violate other people's rights. It has to be done lovingly, openly, and also with a willingness to accept the consequences. And then it really has to be explained, and the counterarguments have to be engaged.

I'll make another point about effects. I'm really just riffing on what Cornel said here: if you're going to do it, you have to realize that you're always risking sending a message that our cause is so important and the injustices we're fighting against are so terrible that extreme measures, such as rapes and murders, are justified. To me, the most upsetting part of what I've been seeing—and this is by no means all the people who have been engaged in protesting, whether at Princeton, on the streets in cities, or at other universities—is when people try to rationalize or fail to acknowledge what happened on October 7, when Hamas murdered, raped, tortured, burned, and kidnapped innocent people. And I fear the sense that there are grave injustices here that have to be rectified, if we're not careful about how we characterize things, can lead people to think that extreme measures are justified—and extreme measures that involve injustices to other people are never justified. I think you agree with that, Cornel, don't you?

West: Absolutely. One of the signs of overwhelming decadence is when the sort of thing you're talking about cannot find a footing because the soil has become so barren. The only places that become available are precisely where it's all about power, contempt, and hatred. One of the problems of any empire occurs when it reaches the point where it is so far removed from the best of itself and on intimate terms with the worst of itself, and it feels the only major choices it has are versions of the worst. People like Martin Luther King Jr. or Fannie Lou Hamer or Rabbi Heschel are so far removed to the margin that they are less and less part of the options available to people. It's the same thing in music. If all you had heard was a mediocre voice, and you had never heard Ella Fitzgerald, Sarah Vaughan, Nat King Cole, Frank Sinatra, or Billie Holiday, you would think that the top ten on the pop charts right now represent the height of excellence. That's a sign of profound decadence.

Now transfer that to our politics. What we're talking about with King and the others is just so far outside. When you try to build on that legacy, you discover, lo and behold, these seeds are not sprouting because there's very little soil left. That's the sign of an empire that's imploding. I'm not saying that's an accurate description of the present. I'm just saying that's the dominant orientation. We've still got wonderful fellow citizens of all colors, genders, sexual orientations, religious identities, and non-religious identities, but the very folk we're talking about feel impotent. When JFK said, "Those who make peaceful revolution impossible will make violent revolution inevitable," that is what I find frightening at the moment. And yet you could argue that has been the case for almost every moment in the history of the species. Societies and empires have different cycles of development and emergence, but that's just who we are as a species. That's one of the reasons why we've tried to talk about the humanities and humanistic inquiry at its deepest level, from Plato to Kafka to Ralph Ellison to Saul Bellow; the great artists who have raised these deep, perennial, profound questions. Life, death, joy, sorrow—when their voices are pushed to the margin, we are just left with versions of Thrasymachus. And at that point, what do you do?

George: Life is tragic. I'm reminded by what you're saying, Cornel, of Gandhi's witness. We celebrate Gandhi today, but he was very controversial, of course, in his own time. He was the great model for King of nonviolent revolution in his efforts to overthrow British imperial rule in India. He believed it could be done without unleashing the Hindu versus Muslim violence that ended up being one of the great tragedies of the twentieth century, with an enormous death toll and lasting consequences of hatred and bitterness. So even as we celebrate Gandhi for his moral witness, we have to realize that in one very important respect, despite his best efforts, he failed. He was not able to produce a united India. Instead, we got the division, the partition with violence, bloodshed, and bitterness. And this story is still not over.

Many young people today feel that American society is deeply unfair or unjust, particularly around the issue of racial injustice or structural racism. A lot of people respond to this by saying, "But I don't feel any prejudice." But then they're told that racism isn't a matter of your personal feelings or beliefs; you are simply racist by virtue of participating in a racially discriminatory system. This leads to a number of seemingly difficult to understand propositions, such as that a Black person cannot be racist, because they don't have institutional power. But that description doesn't seem to apply to every individual in our society, including many Black people in positions of power and influence. What do we do with these anomalies, where there seems to be truth on both sides?

West: Malcolm X said at the very end of his life, "I'm for truth, no matter who tells it. I'm for justice, no matter who it is for or against. I'm a human being, first and foremost, and as such I'm for whoever and whatever benefits humanity as a whole." And he said, I'm a Black man and I'm a Muslim. That's humanistic discourse. So, that acknowledges, for example, that Black people have always had power. Every oppressed group always has power.

There's a wonderful play by Arthur Miller, who talks about Jewish brothers and sisters in the concentration camps, still playing beautiful music. That's a spiritual power that the vicious Nazis could not completely eliminate. Likewise, you don't produce some of the most beautiful melodies in the history of the species, under 244 years of barbaric slavery, without enslaved Africans also having that kind of spiritual power. And certainly, these days, if I came up and slapped a white brother upside the head for no good reason, just because he's white, that's an expression of both prejudice and power. That's a racist act.

Now, I might not have that much power on Wall Street. I might not have that much power in the bureaucracy of the state. But the point is, human beings always have responsibility. Because they always have power. They always have agency. They also have innate human dignity, but they can still be victimized in a variety of ways. I say the same thing about women, the same thing about gay brothers, lesbian sisters, trans, whoever. But Malcolm X's humanistic discourse at the very end—similar to King, similar to Rabbi Heschel, and a whole host of others—today that's weakening. It's becoming feeble.

One of the things that Brother Robby and I have always tried to accent as teachers is the famous line in the letter that the great Henry James wrote in 1901 to that other great brother, Robert Louis Stevenson. James said that no theory is kind to us that cheats us of seeing. No theory is kind to us that cheats us of seeing. So, if you come in with identity politics and you're seeing race, race, race, race, race, you're being cheated. You're not seeing other dimensions, other phenomena at work.

George: But look at the other side of that. At the same time, and not accidentally, Cornel is speaking up for human universality. See, there are the two sides. It's because we recognize the profound and inherent and equal dignity of each and every human being that we must treat each and every one as an individual person and not reduce him to the status of being simply a member of this or that group, where our concern or lack of concern is justified by that person's group membership as we categorize that person.

West: Absolutely.

George: Well, those who have embraced, fully and enthusiastically embraced, identity politics, will tend to divide the world up into classes of persecuted and persecutors, victims and victimizers, the powerful and the powerless, as determined by identities other than, for example, socioeconomic class. So, in the new identitarian ideology, the white Appalachian coal miner's daughter is in the oppressor or persecutor class, and the Black or Latino banker's son from Westchester or Scarsdale is in the victim or persecuted class. The categories that are determinative are the ones having to do with race and sex. And there are obvious problems with this—

West: Absolutely.

George: But for people who are in the grip of this ideology, it just seems to be self-evidently true that here's how the world is divided up. And so, all sorts of practices go on in universities that reflect this. You've had orientation sessions at my own university a few years ago in which, at the very beginning, students were asked to identify themselves to the whole of the group, stand up or raise your hand, based on your socio-economic class identities, with some being treated as if they are the persecuted and others as if they're the persecutors.

Our administration wisely put an end to that at Princeton, but it did go on, and it goes on today at lots of other places. And I think that reflects a certain mentality that's being shaped by our ambient politics, which is heavily identitarian on the left and has generated a corresponding identity politics with some elements on the right.

If I could add just one more point. If our students today, especially our students on the left, were introduced to the work of a person of the old left, like Christopher Lasch—let's say they were introduced to his books, like *The Culture of Narcissism* or *The Revolt of the Elites* or *The True and Only Heaven*—I think they would find it offensive. They would find it representative of a kind of cultural conservatism that they would see as antithetical to their progressive politics.

Even a figure like Adolph Reed, a distinguished scholar of American politics and a self-identified progressive who has been sharply critical of identity politics and anti-racist ideology, wouldn't be considered heretical necessarily, but he would be considered irrelevant. I mean, he's not the kind of person who matters in the way that Ta-Nehisi Coates or Ibram X. Kendi would matter. So, for an earlier generation of people on the left, Reed would be an intellectual leader.

But today, that approach is just considered irrelevant. It's on the sidelines. It's not where the action is. It's not in the progressive mindset as such. Progressives like Cornel, or Reed, or the historian of slavery Eugene Genovese, who later shifted his political views—in the old days, these guys were progressives for sure, and non-identitarians, at least in the contemporary sense. So, it's not something in progressivism as such any more than it's in conservatism as such (though, as I said, you now have some elements within the conservative movement who are more than flirting with identitarianism).

Do you see that kind of identity politics as broadly influential on the right?

George: No, but I worry that it might become so. There are certainly some figures who are getting a lot of attention and attracting a certain amount of sympathy.

Why do radical views always attract so much attention?

George: Well, I think here it's largely reactionary. On my own side, I certainly don't want the identitarians to win. And I noticed that the identitarians, while there are some religious folk among them, and they've even got certain schools of thought that bring religion into it—the so-called Christian nationalist movement, for example—the elements of conservatism that are really in the vanguard and I think attracting the real sympathy on the right tend to be secular, and I think there's a reason for that.

They don't like Christianity's universalism, and they don't like the general universalism of the biblical and Abrahamic traditions, where all human beings share the most fundamental thing. The most fundamental thing about everyone is that we're human beings. That's more fundamental than being American, being Black, being white, being male or female, being Protestant or Catholic or Jewish or Hindu. For these traditions, the most fundamental thing about all of us is, I'm a human being. A moment ago, Cornel quoted Malcolm X from a later period in his life, when he had discovered orthodox Islam. What did he say about himself first? The first thing he said about himself was, "I'm a human being and I'm a Black man and I'm a Muslim."

West: That's right.

George: So, he led with being a human being. And there are elements on the right now that don't lead with being a human being. They lead with something else, being white, being conservative. Weirdly, for those who do have a religious perspective, they'll say, "I'm a Christian." But if you're a Christian, the first thing you should be noticing is the thing I have in common with everybody else, including the non-Christians, which is that I'm a human being, a creature made in the image and likeness of God.

West: But I think it's important to acknowledge that the humanistic tradition that we're talking about has always been a flickering candle against the backdrop of barbarism in the history of the species. I mean, it's not new. We may have elevated our expectations during certain moments of enlightenment, thinking that perfection's just around the corner, utopia can be achieved, and so forth. But these are all illusions. And Christian, Hindu, Buddhist, secular, polytheistic belief systems have always had institutional practices that stood in the way of that deeper moral and spiritual truth that Robby's talking about. In that sense, we must acknowledge a kind of failure of the species.

George: Absolutely.

West: We're right back to a philosophical anthropology. What kind of organism are we? How wretched and terrible are we?

How wonderful and full of dignity and sanctity are we? It's a matter of just keeping track of both of those, it seems to me. So, I'm never—maybe this is the Chekhov and Jesus that's trying to get through me—but I'm never surprised by any form of vicious evil. Never. It's not like I have to read Jonathan Swift or François Rabelais to know that, but they confirm it. But I'm not paralyzed by despair either. You see, I'm not a misanthropist. I don't look only at how ugly things are. Like the late Mark Twain: "that damn human race." I mean, he became like Swift, right? He was misanthropic across the board. And again, I draw a distinction between retail misanthropy and wholesale misanthropy. There's a moment in which all of us look around and say, We human beings are—

George: What's that word you like? Wretched.

West: Exactly.

George: Look within every group, no matter how victimized they've been, you find the same problems. I'll tell you a little story. When my roommate was getting married, I was at the bride's house with the wedding party staying overnight, and I got up early in the morning, and the only person up was the father of the bride. He asked me if I'd like some breakfast, and he made me a nice breakfast. And we were sitting down together. I can remember being outside on a little patio, eating our breakfast together, and he was reflecting. This was his first child to be married. And he said to me, really to himself, but out loud, "In my day, a marriage like this would not have been possible."

I couldn't figure out at first what he meant by that. And I thought, well, both the bride and the groom were Jewish, so it couldn't be that. But I said, "Well, they're both Jewish, right?" He said, "Oh, yeah, they're both Jewish. But in my grandfather's generation, the German Jews like our family would never marry or allow our children to marry Slavic Jews. We wouldn't even be buried in the same cemetery with them." That's within the group, a group that had in so many ways been victimized. And Cornel could tell you all about that same tendency within the Black community.

West: Oh yes.

George: And color—complexion—was right at the heart of it.

West: We human beings—we're just so creative when it comes to evil and when it comes to different labels and stereotypes and categories to rationalize that evil. And so, we just have to be honest and candid about that. That's one of the things we do with our students. We say, "Look, we all look at the world through a set of lenses. All of us have splinters in our eyes." Theodor Adorno used to say, "The splinter in your eye is the biggest magnifying glass." Because you have to come to terms with your own myopia, your own shortsightedness, what you are not seeing, what you are not feeling, cries that you are not hearing, acts that you are not following through on. And the aim of education for both of us, and it is as old as Plato's *Republic*, is how do we see more clearly and feel more deeply and hear more attentively and act more compassionately and courageously before the worms get our bodies?

And that's the great humanist tradition. No one civilization or empire has ever been able to actualize it at the level that we want, but there have been some that are better than others. There have been some great breakthroughs. There have also been some major setbacks in the humanist tradition, and we're living at a moment in which, and I've said this before, the cultural decay and the psychic decadence and the overwhelming conformity and cowardliness that's becoming more and more predominant in our world and in our country, puts us in a new and surprising predicament. But it is what it is. You've got to come to terms with it.

George: I think it's important to point out that in our classes when we're teaching together and we're addressing student audiences or young people, we make it clear, and not just by precept, but in every way we can, that we regard everybody as having something to say and something to learn from others. We won't allow anyone to suppose that because I'm in this category, this identitarian box, my job is to sit and listen and be lectured to by other people, nor do we allow anyone to suppose that because I'm in this other identitarian box, my job is to preach and other people's job is to listen. No. That contradicts both the universalism that we represent and the individualism that we represent, which are necessarily connected to each other. Everybody, irrespective of what category you put them in in terms of race, ethnicity, sex, or religion, has something to say, and others have something to learn from that person, even if it's only the questions that that person has.

Often, we learn from the questions other people raise, not just the answers they give to our questions, and everybody has something to learn from everybody else in the room. So, we want a conversation among people who understand themselves as equal participants. Now, they'll have different backgrounds and perspectives, and those will sometimes be shaped by matters having to do, for example, with their race. Cornel will have had some experiences by virtue of being Black that I don't have.

West: And vice versa.

George: And vice versa. And we welcome that. We don't say, "You can't talk about experiences that you've had in which race is implicated because that is identitarianism, and we're against that." We don't say that. We realize that in this world, sometimes our experiences are what they are, at least in part, because of, for example, race. But what we will not allow is somebody to say, "Because you haven't had my experiences, you are not allowed to question me. You are not allowed to criticize me. You are not allowed to interrogate me. My experiences speak for themselves and are unchallengeable." We don't allow that. We're going to have a real conversation here, and anybody can ask any questions they think are pertinent to ask to learn what there is to be learned.

West: Absolutely. I think the younger generation has a large number of progressives who understand themselves as being tied to struggles against white supremacy, male supremacy, struggles against homophobia and transphobia. They can become preoccupied with one particular issue as it connects to their own particular identity. I think that's in part what Brother Robby means by identity politics. And then there's a smaller slice that is concerned about issues of empire, that are anti-imperialist, and issues of predatory capitalist processes.

But for someone like myself, I begin with William James's conception of education, which asks, "How do you cultivate a habitual vision of greatness, a vision of excellence?" So, when you situate my own tradition, somebody like a Martin Luther

King Jr., or a Fannie Lou Hamer or Dorothy Day, or even an Edward Said, you are really talking about a humanist tradition. That tradition is concerned about the relation of structures of domination, forms of dogma, and various kinds of death—physical death, social death, civic death—in which people are discriminated against as part of the body politic so effectively they're dead.

And so, I tell the students, "Look, there's one fundamental identity. Every human organism has a desire for protection, association, and recognition." Now, if you want that kind of identity politics, you're talking about humanistic politics. You're talking about issues of class, gender, empire, sexual orientation, ethnicity, disability. There's a whole set of categories of people who have not been treated justly and fairly.

So, you end up again, being improvisational. You have young students—let's say like when the students took over the president's office again at Princeton—who were primarily concerned about issues of racism. Well, of course, on moral and spiritual grounds, you're concerned about racism. The same would be true if workers are not being treated. The same would be true of the elders. The same would be true if conservatives are not treated well. The same would be true of anybody who's not been treated well, treated fairly, treated justly.

The question then becomes, how do you intervene with this old left/new left divide, identity politics among the younger generation, a smaller slice still concerned about issues of empire and capitalism? That's part of the challenge when people think, "Well, you got all these Marxists taking over." No, identity politics is really not too Marxist at all, and it's often accommodating itself to the existing class hierarchy and the American empire itself. So, Barack Obama could be an example of identity politics, representing Black Americans, but he's also the head of the empire, and he's dropping more bombs than George Bush. The critique becomes even more intense on that particular front, which I tried to put forward for eight years when he was president.

You can see how identity politics just lends itself to being devoured or being co-opted or being thoroughly incorporated within a class hierarchy when it becomes a debate about how many Black folk are on Wall Street so they can join the greedy club. Which is not to say all Wall Street brothers and sisters are greedy, but it is to say that the culture of Wall Street puts a premium on greed, for the most part.

Even those like Brother Robby—Brother Robby has a moral defense of capitalism that is devastating in its critique of monopoly capitalism, in which the markets are really not free. They're being dominated by these monopolies at the top—

George: I don't myself care much for the word capitalism, but I do believe in markets, and I think that markets are crucial for many reasons, including the one that's usually focused on, which is the importance of freedom. It's also very important for prosperity. I think markets lift people out of poverty, where they're introduced in a circumstance of poverty. But Cornel's absolutely right. There's all the difference in the world between genuine markets and a situation in which powerful economic interests, albeit private, not governmental, can control markets in ways that amount to monopolies and oligopolies, which actually undermine the market and make it impossible to actually confer broadly the benefits that make me a supporter of the market economy.

I also think it's terribly important that the market only be permitted to operate within its legitimate sphere, and the legitimacy is determined by principles of morality. There are some things, in other words, that shouldn't be for sale. Just because there's a market for something doesn't mean that the market for it should be allowed to function. An extreme form of libertarianism—and I'm not accusing all or even most libertarians of being extremists—would equate market outcomes with moral goodness, and that's a terrible mistake. Morality stands in judgment over the market just as morality stands in judgment over every other institution. We have to judge an economic institution, a political institution, an educational institution by reference to principles of morality, including principles of justice.

West: I think part of the problem in our culture is that the distrust and despair in terms of communication breakdown is so pervasive, just like with your infamous *60 Minutes* interview, you lay out your opinion, they still distort it. You lay out very slowly and carefully an argument, it still gets distorted.

George: I recall that episode all too well. I was serving on the President's Council on Bioethics in the 2000s, and was asked to give an interview to Lesley Stahl of CBS's *60 Minutes*. Before my conversation with Stahl, I gave a long "pre-interview" to the producer, who was impressively well-prepared and asked good questions about ethical concerns surrounding embryonic stem-cell research. So, I expected the actual interview for on-air broadcast to be good. But in the event, Stahl was not well-prepared and I had to spend a lot of time correcting erroneous presuppositions of her questions. To make matters worse, the actual filmed interview, when it aired, had been edited in a way that distorted the points I had carefully made about a complex subject whose scientific as well as ethical dimensions needed careful treatment. I was, as they say, fit to be tied—especially since the editing seemed to have been done to advance a certain narrative and agenda.

West: So, you can't have the kind of Socratic dialogue that we call for in a context where the distrust is so overwhelming that the baser aspect of our human natures is going to be uppermost, and the best in us is going to be discarded.

And see, that's the soil for Thrasymachus, right there. Thrasymachus becomes hegemonic in that situation, which is another way of saying fascism becomes the major option for such a culture, for such a society. Because you need a tyrant to impose order, because disorder goes hand in hand with paranoia, goes hand in hand with distrust, goes hand in hand with lack of patience. We don't have patience with each other. "How come you're not agreeing with me after three minutes? I've told you what the truth is." "Hey, it's not self-evident to me." "It's not self-evident to you, what's your problem?"

George: There's something wrong with you, right?

West: Exactly.

George: So, people assume, so often, and this is another problem with identity politics where it prevails, that the only account anyone will be able to give of why someone disagrees with them is that that person must be either an ignoramus or ill-intentioned. That person must be either a fool or a bigot or a hater or something like that. In this context, people will lose the sense that issues are often complicated. Many issues are very difficult, and it's natural and normal for reasonable people of goodwill to disagree. The Heterodox Academy that Cornel and I have both been involved with, an association of scholars representing a wide range of viewpoints organized by social psychologist Jonathan Haidt to promote free inquiry, robust civil discourse, and diverse perspectives, has a wonderful slogan: "Great minds don't all think alike."

That is the human condition. We should expect disagreement. We shouldn't be baffled by it to the point that we have to explain someone's disagreement with us by questioning their motives or their intelligence. Reasonable people of goodwill throughout human history, the greatest minds, have disagreed. Aristotle deeply disagreed with his teacher, Plato, about some very, very important issues.

West: Yes, he did.

George: You'd have a hard time trying to find me two people more brilliant than Plato and Aristotle. Did they come to the same opinions about everything? No. On some things they did, but on some very important things, they did not. Now, why should we expect anything else from ourselves and our fellow citizens?

West: That's true. But when it comes to the ideological challenge, more and more there's a sense that the canonical thinkers somehow reside or tilt toward conservative sensibilities, conservative politics. So that in so many instances in the university, if you find yourself invoking these classical figures, they figure somehow that's a signal for right wing X or Y.

Then someone like me comes along and says, "No, no, no. This classical tradition is mine as well as Robby's." From Socrates to Diderot, to Goethe, to Dante to Du Bois. They are Robby's, and they are also mine. But there's still a sense in the culture that those thinkers are somehow tilting toward the right. This makes it difficult to create bonds of trust and the context of patience that is required for a substantive conversation.

George: Brother Cornel has been criticized by one of his own left wing colleagues for assigning to students the writings of Du Bois. Can you imagine? Du Bois is unacceptable? He's regarded as "right wing" from a certain perspective, and therefore shouldn't even be assigned to students. I mean, this to me represents going through the looking glass. We're now outside the realm of reason, altogether.

Cornel made another very important point, I thought, about the breakdown of trust. To have a conversation, the interlocutors need to trust each other. For institutions to work, there needs to be trust among the people in the institutions. For societies to work, there needs to be some fundamental level of trust in the institutions.

One of the changes that I've seen in my lifetime has been that we've gone from a high degree of trust in our institutions— political, legal, religious, economic, military, social—to a very low level of trust. You see this in our attitude toward government. Do you fundamentally trust the government to do the right thing or to tell you the truth or do you not? When I was a boy in the 1960s, most Americans trusted the government to at least try to do the right thing and to tell them the truth. That has now collapsed. Look at the churches. Look at religion.

Trust in religion and religious leaders used to be high. Now it's low. The military was always among the most highly trusted institutions. Now, trust in the military hasn't fallen quite so far, but it's still down from where it once was.

And here's the worst thing. These institutions have, to a very large degree, earned that distrust.

West: Yes, absolutely.

George: It's not just that people have become cynical for no reason at all. It's the failings of the institutions themselves, which means the failings of the people in the institutions, especially those in authority, that are ultimately responsible for the collapse of trust. But if our society is to survive and flourish, then we are going to need to reform and rebuild those institutions and hope that these reformed and renewed institutions will regenerate the trust that they once enjoyed.

And this goes all the way down to the educational institutions and the relationship between teacher and student and between scholar and scholar. If in our scholarly discourse we're going to make any real progress, we need to be able to trust each other, to have the kinds of serious, sometimes tense discussions and debates that we need to have. It's the same with students and faculty members. Students have to be able to trust the good faith of their teachers. Faculty need to be able to trust their students. Faculty members today live in fear that their students will report something they said, perhaps out of context, which makes them sound, let's say, bigoted. Teachers fear that disaffected students will wage cancellation campaigns against them that could cost them their jobs and their careers.

That makes the teacher too timid to speak in a way that challenges the students and helps them to make intellectual progress. Until we rebuild that basic trust, those students will be denied the advantages that they would have gained if the professor could play his proper Socratic role and not have to worry about the personal consequences of being reported on.

Why is this happening? Why would these students work so hard to get in to a place like Princeton, to have access to all these great teachers, and then look for ways to destroy them?

George: Students are influenced and shaped by the ambient politics and that politics is an identity politics. That means there are "the good guys" and "the bad guys." And you're constantly on the lookout to see if somebody says something that will enable you to identify him as a "bad guy." And then because you've identified him as a "bad guy," you've got to destroy him and make an example of him and get him out of this institution. It's so destructive.

West: But you see, examples can change perception. Somebody could have a perception of Robby as a stereotypical conservative. Then they meet him, they go to his classroom, they have a discussion, and they say, "I was wrong." Stereotypes can be shattered. And I think that's very important to keep in mind, because the students themselves, oftentimes have a certain suspicion that because what Brother Robby says is true, so many of these institutions have earned the crisis of legitimacy, because they haven't come through.

And the only way you cut against that grain is to earn a different kind of status. There's a wonderful memoir by Frank Kermode, the greatest British literary critic of his generation, called *Not Entitled*. It's a beautiful book because he comes out of the artisanal classes, the lower middle working classes of Britain, and talks about his sense of always feeling not entitled. Now, what does Kermode do? He becomes the most respected literary critic in the English language. And it's a status that he earned.

That's one of the things Robby and I both try to do in our own lives. We seek to earn the respect of our adversaries by exemplifying a certain surprising complexity. So, people may say, "Well, Cornel West is a stereotypical white-hating Black man who's obsessed with slavery and Jim Crow." Yes, I am deeply, deeply concerned about the legacy and afterlife of slavery and Jim Crow and Jane Crow and so forth. No doubt. You got the right Black man when you're talking about that.

But then they get a chance to meet me, and they say, "But my God, you're also concerned about Roma, concerned about Jews in Russia, concerned about Palestinians in Gaza and the West Bank, concerned about peasants in Ethiopia. Are you concerned about landless workers in Brazil, Dalits in India, or young women in Iran?" Absolutely. You got the right brother there, too. That's the humanistic tradition, shattering these narrow stereotypes, and the only way you do it is by personal example.

Now, we all fall on our faces, too. So, I'm sure there's a whole lot of people out there saying, "Brother Robby and Brother West don't earn it at all. Stay away from them." But that's part and parcel of what it is to be a human being—and a public intellectual.

Chapter Seven

Seeking Truth Beyond the Classroom

Let's bring the conversation back to Newman and the role of the university. What are the goals of education and how should it prepare young people for the real world?

Robert P. George: In our class, the goal is to impart to students the habits of mind and heart that will enable them to grapple in a truly human way, using their God-given intellects, with the greatest and most important questions. Those are questions of what it means to be a human being. Newman's vision is a vision of learning that is not reduced to conveying information or even imparting specific analytical skills. Those are important; education should include information and the imparting of skills. But there's a deeper learning, which is a non-instrumental vision of education where we're seeking the truth for the sake of the truth. Encouraging students to seek the truth for its own sake, understanding that its fundamental value is intrinsic and not merely instrumental, is at the heart of Newman's vision and it's at the heart of what we do.

Cornel West: And also to give them a sense that they're not the first ones to have to deal with the treacherous tension between particularity and universality. It means, to take Newman as an example, to be a Catholic at a particular moment in the nineteenth century in a colonized Ireland. And, at the same time, to be able to look for some way of transcending the particular situation you find yourself in that connects you with a conversation among those who've been wrestling with that tension.

Part of the problem we've always had—and this is for our whole careers in the academy—is the tension between thinking well and speaking well. Eloquence goes one way and thinking goes another, so that the union of eloquence and wisdom is lost and you get jargon and knowledge. Jargon today has taken over; it's become hegemonic in the academy. That's why most of the texts that are published these days, 85 percent of the footnotes are texts published within the last five years, as if the dead have little to say.

Now, that is about as narrowly oligarchic in time as you can get. If you're not in deep conversation with the dead, you've already cut off your conversation. And if you're talking with the quick, well God bless them, we got some smart folk who are quick and a few who are wise, but jargon has still taken over. Most important—and this is something that Brother Robby and I really hit hard—is the intimate relation of vocation and tradition, of one's calling and one's recalling. That's been lost.

Now, that is a sign of genuine cultural decadence, which was a topic of concern for T.S. Eliot. We talk a lot about Eliot. He means much to both of us, even though he's got politics very different than mine, and his anti-Jewish sensibilities have got to go. Eliot was living in a moment of crisis and catastrophe, and he had to mobilize the best of what was available to him to keep alive, to preserve the excellence that had helped shape him. And then he comes up with his responses. Now, his responses, we can criticize them, but they are...what's the right word? A kind of witness. Let's get biblical about it. It's the exemplary witness of an Eliot or a Martin Luther King or a Rabbi Heschel or whoever you want to talk about.

They had that sense of vocation and tradition, that sense of eloquence and wisdom. And always rooted in their traditions, Judaism and Christianity. It could be secular, it could be whatever the traditions are—the choices that people make and the freedom we have to try to master our traditions in such a way that we subvert the worst in them and preserve the best in them. That is, for me, what it is to be an intellectual. Not an academic or mental analyst. Not just having intelligence engaging in immediate evaluations, but commitment to intellect, which evaluates those evaluations. That's what the calling really is. And it's a joyful thing. It's an adventure. We intentionally named our class "Adventures of Ideas" after Alfred North Whitehead, whose classic text was required reading for every member of the Society of Fellows at Harvard when they founded it in the 1930s.

George: You had to read that book? I'm delighted to know that. It's among the great works of twentieth-century philosophy.

West: Whitehead is one of the greats of the West in the most barbaric century of recorded time, the twentieth century. He was dealing with his understanding of crisis, his understanding of catastrophe. And so, the young folks say, "Oh my God, these are not just isolated icons in some museum." No, these are vital, vibrant voices, and that's why we bring in the jazz thing. An anthem of my own Black folk: lift every voice, not lift every echo. So, if you're an echo, you got your jargon, you got your specialized discourse, and you've got your nice little perch within the academy. But if you're going to be like John Coltrane or Charlie Parker or Mary Lou Williams, better find your voice. You're not going to be an echo. But you can't find your voice unless you bounce it off the voices of the dead and the quick, the best voices of the past.

These days we know that young people would rather *see* sermons than *hear* sermons. If they see it enacted in what Robby and I are doing, by example, that's the key. You're not trying to pontificate or preach. They can see the joy that we have in wrestling with these classic, canonical texts. And they can see where we fall on our faces back to humility and fallibility and fallenness. We share various Christian conceptions of fallenness, which is much darker than just fallibility.

So, it seems that when young people come to you, they're earnest, they have an appetite for knowledge. They respect truth and they seem to need help to figure out their convictions: What do I stand for? What am I willing to fight and die for? It's no accident that we speak of having the courage of our convictions. Do you feel that you're helping them think things through for themselves in this very confusing, complex society with so many competing truth claims and moral arguments made on both sides?

George: The students I teach certainly fit that description, but I think there's some additional features that need to be mentioned. Yes, they're earnest. Yes, they do want to learn. They want to have self-respect, and that's natural and good. They're also ambitious. It's important to mention that. That's not bad in itself, but it's not good in itself either. It's all a question of how it's integrated into the larger tapestry of their lives. They also very, very much want to be accepted, especially by their peers.

All that produces some good things and some bad things. The bad things include the identification of virtue with having correct political views as opposed to having a good character, that is, having a character marked by the virtues, including the virtue of courage. And at the extreme, and this extreme is reached very often these days, people will substitute having correct views for doing anything noble, genuinely noble. They will excuse themselves from making the sacrifices that they should make for other people on the ground that they have correct views. And having correct views makes you a good person.

As I see it—and I know Cornel will agree with me on this because I have seen him in action in the classroom—our role is fundamentally Socratic. Our role is to impart to them the habits of mind and heart, to encourage in them the virtues that will enable them to be, not just for the four years of college or graduate school, but for their entire lives, determined truth seekers and courageous truth speakers.

Now, that necessarily means that we have to impart to them the virtue of intellectual humility founded on the genuine acknowledgement of the truth that they, like the rest of us, are fallible and that they can be wrong, just as we all can be wrong. They, and we, can be wrong, not only about the trivial or minor things in life, but about the big important things, things having to do with human nature, the human good, human rights, human dignity, human destiny.

Now, having said all that, let me repeat that it's not our job to tell them what to think or to persuade them to think as we do. Even though by definition we believe what we believe because we believe it's true, our job is not to get them to share our beliefs. Our job is to empower them to think for themselves more deeply and more critically, which always includes self-critically.

West: Absolutely.

George: Thinking for themselves means that their thought is not generated by peer pressure, by what they read or see on TikTok, by what their friends say, by their fear of being excluded, fear of being canceled, where they actually have the courage to question dominant opinions and to say what they actually think. A great many students today are terrified to do that. They're terrified to think for themselves, and they're really terrified to express an opinion that is out of line with a dominant opinion in the communities in which they desire acceptance. Our job as Socratic teachers is to get them past that. So, there's a certain sense in which we're moral instructors. But it's a specific and not comprehensive sense. It's imparting the virtues that will enable them to be determined truth seekers and courageous truth speakers.

West: And you'll notice he said virtues rather than just values. Because most young people these days, they associate themselves with their values, which are always weaker and more feeble than virtues, which have to do with habitual dispositions to behave in certain ways owing to one's magnanimity or greatness of character. And greatness of character has to do with integrity, honesty, decency that's far beyond what kind of values you have, what kind of political views you have, what kind of correct so-and-so you have, you see. And so, virtue is at a very different level, at the Socratic level.

George: You cannot just teach them with words.

West: Oh, no.

George: As both of us have said, you also have to teach by example. They need to see in you—in us, as teachers—intellectual humility as well as intellectual passion, independence of mind, and courage. They need to see us practicing the virtues we are encouraging in them. They need to see their teachers as determined truth seekers and courageous truth speakers.

West: When they see Robby, they see somebody who embodies Emerson's ideal of self-reliance: the idea that to be great is to be a nonconformist. It is to have an aversion to conformity, not for the sake of nonconformity, but because one has thought for oneself and decided, like our dear brother and student of Emerson, Henry David Thoreau, to march to a different drummer, hearing a different beat as it were. And one of the things Robby and I always talk about in our dialogues with the larger groups is that to be true to ourselves, we have to also be true to all the different lineages and streams and strands that have been shot through us.

Now, I think of myself as someone who comes from a tradition on the underside of modernity, within the American empire, who has tried to stay in contact with the best of the American empire. And one of those products is a jazz-like way of being in the world. Well, what is jazz about? It's about the blues. What is the blues? It is catastrophe lyrically expressed, catastrophe honestly encountered, catastrophe artistically transfigured. That's what the blues is. If you're not going to be honest about catastrophe, you're not going to be a blues person. You're going to be sanitized, sterilized, deodorized. So, catastrophe becomes just little, small problems.

But to be part of a people whose jazz includes a blues dimension means you're going to be with Herman Melville, because *Moby Dick* is about catastrophe. It's not small problems. Ishmael's not out there trying to solve no problems. He's wondering whether he's still alive or not. It's life or death. This is true for any great work of art. I'm just using that example. But that blues dimension is crucial. The same is true with swing, which is the second feature of jazz. It don't mean a thing if it ain't got that swing. You got to come up with a conception of being in the world that's offbeat.

How come? Because if you look at it in a certain way, it's all closure, dark, cave-like, no way out, no way of proceeding. You have to come up with ways of being in the world that don't fit well. Duke Ellington says dissonance is a way of life for Black people. That's how they created this music, not for entertainment, but solely for dissonance. This is the only way you can make it. You got to be in the minor key.

It's embracing, it's learning from, it's wrestling with—but it's also bringing something with you. And then that third element, which is improvisation, which is practical wisdom. How do you make judgments on the spot in light of your mastery or the best mastery you have of the past and the tradition, but also at the same time be spontaneous? One of the greatest legacies of the Socratic tradition is the centrality of practical wisdom. It's not anti-rational, but it's not just theoretical reason either.

George: It's not an algorithm.

West: It's not a formula or an algorithm. It's something that's alive and vital and changing all the time, rooted in a tradition, but also recognizing that sometimes it fails. You're going to have to look to other traditions if you're unable to work it out. But you have to have an openness, a humility, and a fallibility. But also, in the end, a joy. And I keep coming back to this. For Christians the fruit of all faith is not just following a

Palestinian Jew named Jesus. It's the joy. If you don't have joy, something's missing.

George: You've got me thinking about our students now, and our vocation as teachers is *them*. They are what we are focused on, even more than our scholarship. We are both pretty active writers, but we both understand our calling to be teaching.

West: Yes.

George: And there's a certain piety there, because we are trying in our best way to repay our own teachers. We'll never be able to repay them. But the only way we can gesture in the direction of repaying them is to do for our students, or try to do for our students, what they did so magnificently for us.

So, given where our students are going to school—and they're good kids, they're really good kids—most of them are, at this point in their lives, focused on instrumental goals. Getting a great job. And a great job means Goldman Sachs, Cravath, Swaine & Moore, founding a successful start-up, getting on the executive track at a major corporation. That's what they mean by great. They're interested in professional success and even more in the status that comes with it. They're interested in making a lot of money. They're interested in being respected and influential in their communities. They like applause. They've been pleasers their entire lives—you don't get to Princeton or Harvard without pleasing everybody along the way by your performance in school and on tests and in extracurricular activities of the sort that count in the competition for admission to elite colleges and universities. You're climbing that ladder. And sometimes it's a greasy pole. And you're the winner. If you've made it to Princeton or Harvard, then you've won an awful lot of those competitions. So, students are focused on wealth and power and influence and status and applause and celebrity.

And my message to them is the same as my message to my own kids. It's a message I have to remind myself of sometimes, by the way. Those things are good. They're important. I'm not saying they're bad. They matter. But they don't ultimately matter.

There are things that matter and things that *really* matter. The things that matter are things that are worthwhile, but not for their own sakes. Consider material wealth. Money is something you can do a lot of good with. You can create businesses, give people employment, create products and services that people use and appreciate. If you've earned a lot of money, you can be a philanthropist. You can give away money to the best causes. Wealth certainly isn't bad in itself. But neither is it good in itself. And it's the same with status or prestige or influence or celebrity. You can do a lot of good with those things. If you're high status, you can use your status for the good. If you have prestige, if you're a celebrity, you can use your prestige or celebrity for the good. But those things are not good in themselves. They can also be used for evil.

So, the things that really matter, that ultimately matter, are not the things that are merely instrumentally good. The things that really matter are the things that are intrinsically good. The things that have their value, not merely as means to other ends like wealth and status and power and prestige, and celebrity, but things that are good in themselves: friendship, knowledge, faith, beauty, virtue, integrity, honesty, and so forth.

It's not that our students disagree that those are the more important things. If I put it to them just the way I put it to you, they would totally agree. But it's one thing to notionally agree and it's another thing to actually start shifting focus. We need our students to do a bit more self-critical reflection: "Yeah, you know what? I'm spending all my time thinking about how to get an A in this class. How do I do well on my LSAT? How do I get into Stanford Business School or Harvard Law School? How do I get on track for a Supreme Court clerkship? How do I get to Kirkland & Ellis or Cravath or Goldman Sachs?" Too many of our students are so focused on career advancement they're not thinking about the things that *really* matter.

So, that's part of our Socratic project. That's part of our vocation as teachers. It does concern priorities, and in this sense, values. What they should treat as more important than something else. Is wealth important? Yes, certainly. Is it as important as honesty? No. Is social status important? Yes. Is it as important as integrity? No. Is the approval of others important? Yes. Is it as important as truth or beauty? No.

West: Absolutely. I think both Robby and I do have a certain conception of teaching as a calling that takes the form of *kenosis*, self-emptying. Trying to pour into others what has been poured into us, as it has been filtered through us. It goes all the way back to just growing up, to our parents, your parents, my parents. Irene, Clifton, Shiloh Baptist Church, Reverend Cooke, Black Panther party right next door, breakfast programs, going to the prisons. I've been teaching in prisons now for over forty-seven years. And the brothers say, "Brother West, we just love it. You keep pouring." I tell them I'm trying to pour everything from me into you. Why? Because I think it could be worth it. But it could be misleading, too. So, you got to watch yourself. Everything inside of me is not a positive thing.

But when I think of my high school teachers, and then going to Harvard with—Robby knows it—my tutor Robert Nozick, and then ended up studying with Hilary Putnam, with John Rawls and Martin Kilson and Preston Williams and Samuel Beer. And Stanley Cavell, who I taught with for a whole year. I also took a whole year with Hans-Georg Gadamer, when he came from Germany. Another whole year with Alasdair MacIntyre when he was at Boston University. And J.N. Findlay, a great Hegel scholar from Australia. He would take me to lunches and things. Why did he spend the time with a little brother like me? I was doing my homework and stuff. And I was playing a lot of catch-up because I grew up in the ghetto. So, it's not like I'm reading Max Weber at fourteen, you know what I mean? I'm listening to Motown. James Brown. But it was that sense of just them giving themselves.

Then after Princeton with Walter Kaufmann and T.M. (Tim) Scanlon, and Thomas Nagel and Carl Hempel, Richard Rorty, Sheldon Wolin, Sir Arthur Lewis, and Margaret Wilson. I can go on and on and on. These are folk who embraced me. And they put so much inside of me. You know what I mean? It's like, good God. The least I can do is try to pour out some of that tradition that was filtered through them into me. And our students know, when they interact with me, I've got all those teachers inside of me. All of them. And they're contesting each other.

I'm just saying all that to say, what a blessed life. How could one not want to give to the young folk? In many ways, and I think that as teachers we want to say this directly to young people, they've got to take responsibility for trying to be a cause rather than a brand. But also, we have to engage in an indictment of many of their teachers who have not followed through in the way that they should, who have fallen into webs of conformity, who have moved toward jargon-ridden writing, and not wanting to expose young people to the best of these great traditions. Instead, they are obsessed with contemporary discourse that makes them look clever and smart. On many occasions, Robby and I have told the students, let your phones be smart. You be wise. If you just want to be the smartest in the class, I'm not impressed. If you want to be the wisest, oh, now we got a dialogue.

George: All those people in the past instilled in my brother, piety, gratitude. The sense that from whom much has been given, much is expected. You've got to pay it back. You've got to pass on what was given to you. This is not something that Yale can teach you or Dalton can teach you, or Chevy Chase High School can teach you. If mom and dad or the rabbi or the pastor or the priest is not teaching you, or the little league coach or Mrs. Skeduggen in the library. If somebody close to you personally is not teaching you, you are not going to get it. You can't look it up in a book. You can't take special vitamins to get it. It's mom and dad and grandma and grandpa and pastor and priest and rabbi and teacher and coach.

West: That's true. All of us have these experiences. And they're not just words, but living examples.

We're wrapping up here, but the one thing we haven't really talked about is: Why does truth matter?

George: A little while ago I was teaching a seminar with the eminent Civil War historian and Lincoln biographer Allen Guelzo. The course was on the nature and history and purposes of universities. We were both presenting the idea to our students that the university's mission is fundamentally a truth-seeking mission. A university is not just there to prepare you for professional life or give you a credential, or confer a status, or give your parents a sticker that says "Yale" for the back of the BMW. It's there so that students and faculty members can be about the business of pursuing truth.

And as we discussed that with the students, I detected a division in the class. To crystallize the division and force students to confront the issue and see where they stood on it, I put the following question to them.

"I'm going to give you all two options and each of you can tell me which you choose," I said. "Option A, I will give you a fallacious argument for a true proposition. But my argument, though fallacious, you will find convincing and therefore you will believe the proposition which you hitherto had not believed. Option B, I'll give you a sound argument, a valid argument for the same true proposition, but my argument, though valid and sound, will not be fully persuasive to you, as a result of which you will not embrace the proposition. Do you want A or B? You tell me."

The class divided right down the middle. Half of them said, "I'll take A in a heartbeat. I just want to have true beliefs in my head." The other half of the class were scandalized by that and said, "No, give me the sound argument. Let me wrestle with it even though it's not going to get me to where I want to be."

The right answer is Option B. And that's because the truth is not just propositions in our head. We need not just to know the truth in the sense of affirming the right propositions. We need to *appropriate* the truth. We need to understand not only *that* something is the case, but why it is the case, or how it is the case, or maybe even the deeper significance of it being the case, how it lines up with other things that are the case, other truths. The truth does fulfill us as the kinds of creatures we are, rational beings. We are by nature truth-seeking, truth-attaining creatures. And that seeking and attaining the truth is an aspect of our fulfillment, our integral flourishing. But that fulfillment does not consist in merely having ideas that happen to be correct mainlined into our head.

You can probably guess what my next question would be to the students who chose Option A and who wanted the fallacious argument, so long as it led them to affirm a true proposition. My next question was: "Why bother with going through all the time and effort of making an argument? I've got a pill here. I'll give you the pill. You will now believe the true proposition. No argument, no reasoning. I'll give you the pill."

The idea of the pill is familiar to most people. Cornel was in *The Matrix* movies, where there's that famous scene with the red pill and the blue pill. The point made there is a good one: It is in our nature and for our good to be in touch with reality. Even when it hurts. It is contrary to our nature as human beings, contrary to our good, to be out of touch with reality—to take the pill that lands or keeps us in an imaginary world.

What we have learned from the great teachers of humanity, East and West, Socrates, Jesus, going all the way up to our present day, is that it's better to live in the real world with full knowledge than it is to live in a world of illusion. The Harvard philosopher Robert Nozick invited us to consider whether we would choose to plug into what he called the Experience Machine. If the options were to either live in the real world with all its heartaches and joys, or to hook into the Experience Machine where we would spend the rest of our lives, lying in a tank, living in a dream state where we were having every pleasant experience we could imagine, which would we choose?

When Nozick published *Anarchy, State, and Utopia* in 1975, he could count on people saying, "I would not plug into the machine." He could count on people to have that basic insight that is sometimes captured in the aphorism that "it's better to be Socrates dissatisfied, than to be a pig satisfied." In other words, it's better to fulfill our nature as rational creatures than to live as a brute animal.

People like Cornel and myself would not plug into the Experience Machine; we want the red pill. We want to live in the world of reality with all its troubles and heartaches. We can see that it is worth being a human being and that we are not living humanly if we opt for un-reality. My worry is that many people today, especially young people, would not see the point of not plugging into the machine. In an age of feeling, when all that matters is how you feel, and your rationality, your very human nature has been largely effaced, it will not be obvious to people that the superior life is the life in the real world, as opposed to living in a dream or living in illusions.

That temptation could come sooner rather than later, given the technology that motivates people who proclaim themselves to be transhumanists. This could be a real choice, and not just a thought experiment at some time not too far down the line. But for me, it's good to be human.

West: One of the big differences between Nozick in 1975 and where we are now is the transformation of culture, in which more people would say, "I would choose that Experience Machine." There's no doubt about it.

George: When I first read that book in 1976, I read it for a seminar. It was a knockdown. It was considered an argument stopper.

West: Right, right.

George: Everyone agreed that plugging into the machine would be a horrible thing. It'd be a nightmare, even though it would give you pleasant dreams. You'd be in a pleasant dream state, but the reality would be you'd be in a nightmare.

I now wonder how many people would say, "Yeah, that's the good life. That's the life worth living." Even though you're actually not living a life. You're just having a flow of experiences.

West: It's true. America is unique among empires in that it believed it moved from perceived innocence to corruption without a mediating stage of maturity. Every nation-state, every empire, is tied to barbarism, but very few nation-states view themselves as innocent. That's distinctively American. A certain denial of reality, a denial of temporality, and even denial of forms of death. F. Scott Fitzgerald says, "Gatsby believed in the green light," the light he saw across the water, which symbolized his dream of wealth and status, of achieving the American dream. Chekhov didn't believe in the green light. Dostoevsky didn't believe in the green light. Even Saul Bellow—that complicated Russian, Jewish, Canadian, Chicagoan, and New Yorker—he got enough of a tragicomic sensibility to demystify the green light talk.

What do we do with our students? We tell them that one condition of truth is to allow suffering to speak, your suffering and the suffering of others. That comes out of Hebrew scripture. Meaning what? Meaning that in fact, truth, inseparable from the other transcendental universals, beauty—

George: —beauty and goodness, and the holy.

West: Right, goodness and the holy. Rilke says beauty ain't nothing but the first touch of terror we can bear in that first elegy. Rilke knew what he was talking about. Beauty is wrestling with reality. Terror is integral to human history. It's integral to reality. It's integral to time, and it's tied to forms of death. In any nation-state where they say they have never had anything to do with terror and coercion, you know they're lying. They're in denial. Tell people the truth.

The same is true with goodness. Goodness is tied to various forms of evil that take the form of callousness. Rabbi Heschel said that the great sin of humanity is indifference. Indifference to evil is more insidious than evil itself. That's the great wisdom that comes out of Hasidic tradition that Rabbi Heschel utters with his own power and eloquence and elegance.

Then there's the holy. What is the holy about? The holy is about reality. It's about wrestling with time, wrestling with history, and being open to something bigger than ourselves, so that the truth, and the beauty, and the goodness—we can add justice—are connected to the holy. Many of our brothers and sisters around the world reject the holy. They reject God talk. They might have sacred values, but they don't have sacred entities. They don't have sacred powers. They're naturalists in that regard, but they still have connection to something bigger than what we call loosely the mundane.

So, in conclusion, to answer your question: When we talk about why truth matters, we're really talking about allowing our precious students full access to the great intellectual traditions that will force them to wrestle with what it means to be human, in their fallible quest for truth, and beauty, and goodness, and the holy. And we are teaching them to do it in this context— the context of an empire that has magnificent possibilities past and present, and very ugly realities past and present, and at the same time is experiencing imperial decay, military overreach, corruption of elites across parties, a sense of helplessness and impotence among citizenry, and scapegoating the most vulnerable, the weak, and the inability to really focus on the most powerful, because they tend to be invisible.

We try to lay it out in such a way that we keep our joy with a smile, with a style, and tell them, we are a blues nation. We've created the blues. Let's cope with the catastrophe with our compassion. In the end, it's about *phronesis*. In the end, it's about *prudentia*. In the end, it's about improvisation within the spiritual and moral dimension. That's the best, not just of America, but the best of our species, and it helps to start with Athens and Jerusalem.

About the Authors

Cornel West is the Dietrich Bonhoeffer Professor of Philosophy and Christian Practice at Union Theological Seminary. He is also Class of 1943 Professor of African American Studies Emeritus at Princeton University. He is a magna cum laude graduate of Harvard College and obtained his MA and PhD in philosophy at Princeton. Professor West is best known for his classics *Race Matters* and *Democracy Matters*. His memoir is entitled *Brother West: Living and Loving Out Loud*. He made his film debut in the *Matrix*—and was the commentator (with Ken Wilber) on the official trilogy released in 2004. He has made several spoken word albums including *Never Forget*, collaborating with Prince, Jill Scott, André 3000, Bootsy Collins, and others. In 2021, he won a Grammy Award along with Arturo O'Farrill for the year's best Latin jazz album. Professor West has a passion to share and keep alive the legacy of Martin Luther King Jr.—a legacy of telling the truth and bearing witness to love and justice.

Robert P. George is McCormick Professor of Jurisprudence and Director of the James Madison Program in American Ideals and Institutions at Princeton University. He has served as Chairman of the US Commission on International Religious Freedom and on the US Commission on Civil Rights and the US President's Council on Bioethics. He has also been the US member of UNESCO's World Commission on the Ethics of Scientific Knowledge and Technology. He was a Judicial Fellow at the US Supreme Court, where he received the Justice Tom C. Clark Award. A Phi Beta Kappa graduate of Swarthmore, he holds the degrees of JD and MTS from Harvard University and the degrees of DPhil, BCL, DCL, and DLitt from Oxford University. He is a recipient of the US Presidential Citizens Medal and the President's Award for Distinguished Teaching at Princeton University. He is of counsel to the law firm of Robinson & McElwee and a member of the Council on Foreign Relations.